THE
NEWBERY
&
CALDECOTT
AWARDS

A Guide to the
Medal and Honor Books

2015 EDITION

ASSOCIATION FOR LIBRARY
SERVICE TO CHILDREN

AMERICAN LIBRARY ASSOCIATION
CHICAGO   2015

Cover illustration for *The Crossover*, written by Kwame Alexander, reproduced by permission of Houghton Mifflin Harcourt. Cover illustration for *El Deafo*, written by Cece Bell, reproduced by permission of Amulet Books/ABRAMS. Cover illustration for *Brown Girl Dreaming*, written by Jacqueline Woodson, reproduced by permission of Penguin Group (USA). Cover illustration for *The Adventures of Beekle: The Unimaginary Friend*, written and illustrated by Dan Santat, reproduced by permission of Little, Brown/Hachette. Cover illustration for *Nana in the City*, written and illustrated by Lauren Castillo, reproduced by permission of Clarion/Houghton Mifflin Harcourt. Cover illustration for *The Noisy Paint Box: The Colors and Sounds of Kandinsky's Abstract Art*, written by Barb Rosenstock and illustrated by Mary GrandPré, reproduced by permission of Random House Children's Books. Cover illustration for *Sam & Dave Dig a Hole*, written by Mac Barnett and illustrated by Jon Klassen, reproduced by permission of Candlewick Press. Cover illustration for *Viva Frida*, written and illustrated by Yuyi Morales, reproduced by permission of Neal Porter Books/Roaring Brook Press/Macmillan Children's Publishing Group. Cover illustration for *The Right Word: Roget and His Thesaurus*, written by Jen Bryant and illustrated by Melissa Sweet, reproduced by permission of Eerdmans Books for Young Readers. Cover illustration for *This One Summer*, written by Mariko Tamaki and illustrated by Jillian Tamaki, reproduced by permission of First Second/Macmillan Children's Publishing Group.

Printed in the United States of America

19 18 17 16 15   5 4 3 2 1

While extensive effort has gone into ensuring the reliability of the information in this book, the publisher makes no warranty, express or implied, with respect to the material contained herein.

ISBN: 978-0-8389-1326-0
ISSN: 1070-4493

♾ This paper meets the requirements of ANSI/NISO Z39.48-1992 (Permanence of Paper).

Book design in Adobe Caslon Pro. Cover image (c) LilKar/Shutterstock.

Contents

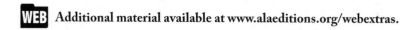   Additional material available at www.alaeditions.org/webextras.

Preface

Welcome to the 2015 edition of *The Newbery and Caldecott Awards*. We are pleased to present the newly minted Newbery and Caldecott Medal titles and Honor Books, along with all those that came before. This compendium represents the most distinguished contributions to American children's literature over the past ninety-plus years.

Reissued each year, *The Newbery and Caldecott Awards* provides a complete listing of winners from the awards' inceptions in 1922 (Newbery Medal) and 1938 (Caldecott Medal). Each edition also includes an essay that delves further into the realm of children's literature. This year, Julie Danielson, author of the popular blog *Seven Impossible Things Before Breakfast*, and co-author of *Wild Things: Acts of Mischief in Children's Literature* (Candlewick, 2014), explores noteworthy picture book imports of recent years—titles originally published in other countries that have made their way to the States, comparing and contrasting them to Caldecott Medal- and Honor-winning books from years past.

Bette J. Peltola's essay, "Newbery and Caldecott Awards: Authorization and Terms," revised by Diane Foote in 2010, discusses terms, criteria, and definitions that have evolved for both awards. The essay continues to provide insight into the significance of the awards and the evaluation of children's literature, while answering the most frequently asked questions about the awards.

Also included within these pages are photos of the 2015 Newbery and Caldecott Medalists and remarks from the award selection committee chairs, which provide some insight into why this year's winners were selected. Information on art media used to create the Caldecott Medal and Honor Books accompanies each individual title.

We hope you find the 2015 guide beneficial, and we welcome your suggestions for future editions.

AIMEE STRITTMATTER
Executive Director
Association for Library Service to Children

Newbery and Caldecott Awards

AUTHORIZATION AND TERMS

Bette J. Peltola, revised by Diane Foote

E ach year the Newbery and Caldecott Medals and Honors are awarded by the
American Library Association for the most distinguished American children's
books published the previous year. Both awards were founded by Frederic G. Melcher,
an influential American bookseller and publisher who served as editor of *Publishers
Weekly* from 1918 to 1933 and eventually served as president and chairman of the board
of the magazine's publisher, R. R. Bowker. The awards are administered by the Association for Library Service to Children, a division of the American Library Association.

The Newbery was first awarded in 1922, after Melcher in 1921 proposed to
the ALA meeting of the Children's Librarians' Section that a medal be given for
the most distinguished children's book of the year. He suggested that it be named
for the eighteenth-century English bookseller John Newbery. In Melcher's formal
agreement with ALA, the purpose of the Newbery Medal was stated as follows: "To
encourage original and creative work in the field of books for children. To emphasize
to the public that contributions to the literature for children deserve similar recognition to poetry, plays, or novels. To give those librarians, who make it their life work
to serve children's reading interests, an opportunity to encourage good writing in this
field." The Newbery Medal thus became the first children's book award in the world.

In 1937 Melcher suggested, and ALA approved, a second annual medal, this
to be given to the artist who had created the most distinguished picture book of
the year and to be called the Caldecott Medal in honor of Randolph Caldecott, the
nineteenth-century English illustrator. The Caldecott Medal "shall be awarded to
the artist of the most distinguished American Picture Book for Children published
in the United States during the preceding year. The award shall go to the artist, who
must be a citizen or resident of the United States, whether or not he be the author of
the text. Members of the Newbery Medal Committee will serve as judges. If a book

---

BETTE J. PELTOLA is professor emerita, School of Education, University of Wisconsin–
Milwaukee.

of the year is nominated for both the Newbery and Caldecott Awards the committee shall decide under which heading it shall be voted upon, so that the same title shall not be considered on both ballots." In 1977 the ALSC Board of Directors rescinded the final part of the 1937 action and approved that "any book published in the preceding year shall be eligible to be considered for either award or both awards." Separate committees to choose the Newbery and Caldecott Medals were established in 1978 and began with the 1980 selection committees.

Changes in Terms for the Awards

A resolution by the Section for Library Work with Children in 1932 that "the book of a previous [Newbery] award winner shall receive the award only upon the unanimous vote" of the committee was rescinded in 1958 by the Children's Services Division. The board of directors stated, "In view of the fact that a unanimous vote in the case of a previous winner of the Newbery or Caldecott Awards was first instituted to encourage new authors and illustrators at a period when such encouragement was needed and since such need is no longer apparent, the restriction of a unanimous vote for winning either award more than once [is] removed from terms for selection [of the awards]." In 1963 the Children's Services Division voted that "joint authors shall be eligible" for the awards.

Also in 1932, the Section for Library Work with Children, with Melcher's approval, adopted the following: "To be eligible for the Newbery Medal books must be original, or, if traditional in origin, the result of individual research, the retelling and reinterpretation being the writer's own."

From the beginning, committees could, and usually did, cite other books as worthy of attention. Such books were referred to as runners-up. In 1971 the term "runners-up" was changed to "honor books." The new terminology was made retroactive so that all runners-up are now referred to as Newbery or Caldecott Honor Books.

In 1978 the ALSC board approved the presentation of certificates to the authors of the Newbery Honor Books and the illustrators of the Caldecott Honor Books. Certificates were presented for the first time in 1986.

Also in 1978, the ALSC board adopted new statements of terms, definitions, and criteria for each award to provide further clarification of the basis on which the awards are to be given. These statements were slightly modified in 1985 and 1987. An Award Eligibility Task Force was convened in 2007 and its recommendations approved in 2008. While the awards' terms and criteria remained the same, the definitions were updated in 2009 to reflect these recommendations. In addition, an "Expanded Definitions and Examples" appendix is available in current editions of the individual award manuals.

Award Committees

The committees that select the Newbery and Caldecott Medal–winning and honor books each have fifteen members including the chair. The ALSC membership elects eight members from a slate drawn up by the ALSC Nominating Committee; the ALSC president-elect appoints the remaining six members; and the ALSC president appoints the chair. All members of the committees are members of ALSC.

During the year, each committee member reads as many of the eligible books as possible, including all books suggested by other committee members and by other members of ALSC. Three times in the autumn, committee members cast preliminary ballots to begin to focus attention on the books likely to be of most interest in the selection discussions. During the selection meetings, the committee discusses all nominated books before beginning balloting. Each committee member votes for three books, with four points assigned to first choice, three to second, and two to third. To win, a book must receive at least eight first-place choices and at least eight points more than any other book. Once a winner is chosen, the committee decides whether to name honor books and how many.

Medals and Seals

Rene Paul Chambellan designed both the Newbery and Caldecott Medals. The bronze medals, shown on pages 8 and 9, have the winner's name and the date engraved on the back. The inscription on the Newbery Medal still reads "Children's Librarians' Section," the section of ALA originally charged with administering the Newbery, although the section has changed its name four times and its membership now includes both school and public library children's librarians—in contrast to the years 1922–58, when the section, under three different names, included only public library children's librarians. (The section names: until 1929, Children's Librarians' Section; 1929–42, Section for Library Work with Children; 1942–58, Children's Library Association; 1958–77, Children's Services Division; and, 1977 to the present, Association for Library Service to Children.)

At the inception of the Caldecott Medal in 1937, the Section for Library Work with Children invited the School Libraries Section (now the American Association of School Librarians) to name five of its members to the awards committee each year. For this reason the Caldecott Medal inscription reads: "Awarded annually by the Children's and School Librarians Sections of the American Library Association." In 1958 the Children's Services Division Board of Directors recognized that the wording on both medals was incorrect in terms of current ALA terminology but decided to retain the original wording on the medals.

Gold (for medal-winning books) and silver (for honor books) facsimile seals may be placed on winning books, either by publishers or by librarians, booksellers, or individuals who already have the books on their shelves at the time the awards are announced. The gold and silver facsimile seals are sold by ALA, with profits going to support the programs and services of ALSC. Permission for photographic reproduction of the seals is also controlled by ALA; profits from commercial reproduction also support the division.

A Time-Honored Tradition

Although some procedures have changed over the years the awards have been given, and some rules or aspects of what the awards are for have been clarified or modified, the basic purpose of honoring distinguished American children's books has not changed. Throughout the years, numerous committees have studied virtually every aspect of the award-giving procedure as well as the rationale and impact of the awards. Such study is likely to continue and ensures a vital life to these awards that have had such an impact on the quality of American literature for children.

John Newbery Medal

The terms, definitions, and criteria for the Newbery Medal are as follows:

Terms

1. The Medal shall be awarded annually to the author of the most distinguished contribution to American literature for children published by an American publisher in the United States in English during the preceding year. There are no limitations as to the character of the book considered except that it be original work. Honor books may be named. These shall be books that are also truly distinguished.
2. The Medal is restricted to authors who are citizens or residents of the United States.
3. The committee in its deliberations is to consider only the books eligible for the award, as specified in the terms.

Definitions

1. "Contribution to American literature" indicates the text of a book. It also implies that the committee shall consider all forms of writing—fiction, nonfiction, and poetry. Reprints, compilations, and abridgments are not eligible.
2. A "contribution to American literature for children" shall be a book for which children are an intended potential audience. The book displays respect for children's understandings, abilities, and appreciations. Children are defined as persons of ages up to and including fourteen, and books for this entire age range are to be considered.
3. "Distinguished" is defined as:
   - marked by eminence and distinction; noted for significant achievement
   - marked by excellence in quality
   - marked by conspicuous excellence or eminence
   - individually distinct

4. "Author" may include coauthors. The author(s) may be awarded the medal posthumously.

5. The term "original work" may have several meanings. For purposes of these awards, it is defined as follows:

   - "Original work" means that the text was created by this writer and no one else. It may include original retellings of traditional literature, provided the words are the author's own.
   - Further, "original work" means that the text is presented here for the first time and has not been previously published elsewhere in this or any other form. Texts reprinted or compiled from other sources are not eligible. Abridgments are not eligible.

6. "In English" means that the committee considers only books written and published in English. This requirement *does not* limit the use of words or phrases in another language where appropriate in context.

7. "American literature . . . published . . . in the United States" means that books first published in previous years in other countries are not eligible. Books published simultaneously in the United States and another country may be eligible. Books published in a U.S. territory or U.S. commonwealth are eligible.

8. "Published . . . during the preceding year" means that the book has a publication date in that year, was available for purchase in that year, and has a copyright date no later than that year. A book might have a copyright date prior to the year under consideration but, for various reasons, was not published until the year under consideration. If a book is published prior to its year of copyright as stated in the book, it shall be considered in its year of copyright as stated in the book. The intent of the definition is that every eligible book be considered, but that no book be considered in more than one year.

9. "Resident" specifies that the author has established and maintains a residence in the United States, a U.S. territory, or a U.S. commonwealth, as distinct from being a casual or occasional visitor.

10. The term "only the books eligible for the award" specifies that the committee is not to consider the entire body of work of an author or whether the author has previously won the award. The committee's decision is to be made following deliberation about the books of the specified calendar year.

Criteria

1. In identifying "distinguished contribution to American literature," defined as text, in a book for children,

   a. Committee members need to consider the following:
   - interpretation of the theme or concept
   - presentation of information including accuracy, clarity, and organization
   - development of a plot

- delineation of characters
- delineation of a setting
- appropriateness of style

Note: Because the literary qualities to be considered will vary depending on content, the committee need not expect to find excellence in each of the named elements. The book should, however, have distinguished qualities in all of the elements pertinent to it.

    b. Committee members must consider excellence of presentation for a child audience.

2. Each book is to be considered as a contribution to American literature. The committee is to make its decision primarily on the text. Other components of a book, such as illustrations, overall design of the book, etc., may be considered when they make the book less effective.

3. The book must be a self-contained entity, not dependent on other media (i.e., sound or film equipment) for its enjoyment.

Note: The committee should keep in mind that the award is for literary quality and quality presentation for children. The award is not for didactic content or popularity.

Caldecott Medal

The terms, definitions, and criteria for the Caldecott Medal are as follows:

Terms

1. The Medal shall be awarded annually to the artist of the most distinguished American picture book for children published by an American publisher in the United States in English during the preceding year. There are no limitations as to the character of the picture book except that the illustrations be original work. Honor books may be named. These shall be books that are also truly distinguished.

2. The award is restricted to artists who are citizens or residents of the United States. Books published in a U.S. territory or U.S. commonwealth are eligible.

3. The committee in its deliberations is to consider only the books eligible for the award, as specified in the terms.

Definitions

1. A "picture book for children," as distinguished from other books with illustrations, is one that essentially provides the child with a visual experience. A picture book has a collective unity of story line, theme, or concept, developed through the series of pictures the book comprises.

2. A "picture book for children" is one for which children are an intended potential audience. The book displays respect for children's understandings, abilities, and appreciations. Children are defined as persons of ages up to and including fourteen, and picture books for this entire age range are to be considered.

3. "Distinguished" is defined as:
   - marked by eminence and distinction; noted for significant achievement
   - marked by excellence in quality
   - marked by conspicuous excellence or eminence
   - individually distinct

4. The artist is the illustrator or co-illustrators. The artist may be awarded the medal posthumously.

5. The term "original work" may have several meanings. For purposes of these awards, it is defined as follows:
   - "Original work" means that the illustrations were created by this artist and no one else.
   - Further, "original work" means that the illustrations are presented here for the first time and have not been previously published elsewhere in this or any other form. Illustrations reprinted or compiled from other sources are not eligible.

6. "American picture book . . . published . . . in the United States" means that books first published in previous years in other countries are not eligible. Books published simultaneously in the United States and another country may be eligible. Books published in a U.S. territory or U.S. commonwealth are eligible.

7. "In English" means that the committee considers only books written and published in English. This requirement *does not* limit the use of words or phrases in another language where appropriate in context.

8. "Published . . . during the preceding year" means that the book has a publication date in that year, was available for purchase in that year, and has a copyright date no later than that year. A book might have a copyright date prior to the year under consideration but, for various reasons, was not published until the year under consideration. If a book is published prior to its year of copyright as stated in the book, it shall be considered in its year of copyright as stated in the book. The intent of the definition is that every eligible book be considered, but that no book be considered in more than one year.

9. "Resident" specifies that the artist has established and maintains a residence in the United States, a U.S. territory, or a U.S. commonwealth, as distinct from being a casual or occasional visitor.

10. The term, "only the books eligible for the award" specifies that the committee is not to consider the entire body of work of an artist or whether the artist has previously won the award. The committee's decision is to be made following deliberation about books of the specified calendar year.

The Medal Artwork

*John Newbery
Medal front (top)
and back*

The Caldecott Medal front (top) and back

Criteria

1. In identifying a "distinguished American picture book for children," defined as illustration, committee members need to consider:

   - excellence of execution in the artistic technique employed
   - excellence of pictorial interpretation of story, theme, or concept
   - appropriateness of style of illustration to the story, theme, or concept
   - delineation of plot, theme, characters, setting, mood, or information through the pictures
   - excellence of presentation in recognition of a child audience

2. The only limitation to graphic form is that the form must be one which may be used in a picture book. The book must be a self-contained entity, not dependent on other media (i.e., sound, film, or computer program) for its enjoyment.

3. Each book is to be considered as a picture book. The committee is to make its decision primarily on the illustration, but other components of a book are to be considered especially when they make a book less effective as a children's picture book. Such other components might include the written text, the overall design of the book, etc.

Note: The committee should keep in mind that the award is for distinguished illustrations in a picture book and for excellence of pictorial presentation for children. The award is not for didactic intent or for popularity.

Storytelling
across Borders

Julie Danielson

In her 2014 Batchelder Award acceptance speech, editorial director and publisher Claudia Zoe Bedrick of Enchanted Lion Books eloquently described the reasons for bringing children's books from other countries to American shores. Among those reasons is "the chance to develop a more nuanced and more inclusive view of the world, a view extending far beyond both the mental and physical boundaries of one's own culture" (Bedrick 2014a). It is for this reason and many others that I like to keep my eye on picture books from other continents that are published here in the United States.

There are some fundamental differences in storytelling in picture books that originate from other countries, as compared to American ones. These differences can illuminate what it is that we, as American readers, value in picture books. Often, we want a story that speaks to our culture, so what is it that our culture values? What do the committee members of the American Library Association's Youth Media Awards choose compared to what is published in other countries? These choices can work as a mirror to reflect what the American gatekeepers of children's literature find worthwhile.

It's easy to over-generalize, but a review and comparison of recent picture book imports to recent Caldecott winners and Honor books suggest that Americans tend to prefer tidy endings, a clear resolution to a story in the 32 or 40 pages of a picture book, whereas, on the whole, many picture book imports seem more comfortable

---

JULIE DANIELSON writes about picture books at *Kirkus Reviews, BookPage,* and her own site, *Seven Impossible Things Before Breakfast.* She is one of the authors of *Wild Things: Acts of Mischief in Children's Literature,* released in 2014, and she also teaches a picture book course for the University of Tennessee's School of Information Sciences graduate program.

with open endings and ambiguities. Picture book imports also tend to deal more frequently with the emotional and even existential challenges children face, including death. Often these two things—imports' lack of perfect clarity in story resolutions and their willingness to address life's mysteries and challenges—go hand in hand.

For the purposes of this discussion, I will look at picture books originally published in other countries, which then are translated (if applicable) and published here in the States, often years later, as first American editions or the equivalent. I will focus on outstanding picture book imports from the past several years, relying (but not solely) on the United States Board on Books for Young People's (USBBY) Outstanding International Books Lists, and compare and contrast them to Caldecott winners from the year 2000 to the present. While the Caldecott Award is given to artists, I'll discuss narrative differences, for the texts of Caldecott-winning books are generally considered to be among the best examples of storytelling in American picture books. Further, artistic styles and schools of art do not necessarily conform to borders. I will sometimes incorporate the thoughts of various editors and publishers with whom I corresponded via e-mail—those who make an effort to publish imported picture books and bring the world to young readers in the United States.

We must pause to discuss the fact that there are blurry lines when we try to define what precisely we mean by "international" picture books. There are those illustrators, for one, originally from other countries but who have US citizenship, whose work is published and revered here in the States, and whose work sometimes retains what some people consider an international flavor—or at the very least they have a style that looks different from many American picture books. Some of these illustrators include Sergio Ruzzier (Italy), Peter Sís (Czech Republic), Yuyi Morales (Mexico), and Vladimir Radunsky (Russia). There are also those illustrators who live overseas, yet their work is consistently published here in the States—that is, not as imports. Their books see first editions in the United States or they are published simultaneously here and in another country. We American readers often see the picture books of Polly Dunbar (England), Bob Graham (Australia), Petr Horáček (born in Prague and now living in England), Meilo So (born in Hong Kong but now in the Shetland Islands), and more. There are even those American illustrators who have studied elsewhere. "Eric Carle's books are so universal that they are published all over the world in countless languages and countries," points out editor Michael Neugebauer, director of publishing for Minedition, based in Hong Kong. "One would not say his books are typically American, [and] we know he studied in Germany. But no one would call his books imports" (Neugebauer 2014). We don't describe Maira Kalman's work as international, yet she was born in Tel Aviv. Despite these blurry lines, we can still make comparisons between imports and homegrown books.

On the whole, imports' tendencies to avoid clear-cut answers, as well as provide open endings, have always seemed to me a marked difference when compared to American picture books. When I asked publishers and editors who make a point of bringing imports to American readers about this, they said the same. "I find [that] a lot of picture books from other countries are more ambiguous," Heather Lennon tells me. Lennon is the managing director of the US division of Switzerland-based NorthSouth Books. "In the United States, we like our themes and our lessons. Those aren't always the best books, but I think that's what many people are used to seeing. So, if the wily fox doesn't get his comeuppance in the end, here in the United States that's not satisfying. In another country, they might say, 'Eh, that's how it is'" (Lennon 2014). Sheila Barry from Groundwood Books responds similarly, saying that many North American picture books tend to follow an overly tidy structure, and "it's refreshing to see books from, say, Argentina or Brazil that do not adhere to a linear way of storytelling in the text or the images. They also tend to be a bit more open-ended than many North American picture books, where every problem needs to be solved by page 32" (Barry 2014).

In looking at some of the more outstanding picture book imports from recent years, we see many examples of this type of storytelling. One of the most recent is cartoonist Ricardo Siri Liniers' *What There Is Before There Is Anything There: A Scary Story*. First published in Argentina in 2006 and brought to American children in 2014 by Groundwood Books, it's the unsettling story of a boy who experiences what could be described as night terrors. In this book, as the boy tries to fall asleep, the ceiling above his head is replaced by a hole, "black and infinite." Strange creatures descend from the ceiling, followed eventually by a "dark and shapeless" presence that tells the boy, "I am what there is before there is anything there" (Liniers 2014, unpaged). The boy's solution is to run to his parents' room. As he lies in their bed, yet another creature falls from the ceiling, indicating that the boy's fears remain. That's the final page of the book. There's no tidy ending, and in fact, there's no resolution to speak of. The *Horn Book* review describes it as "bravely existential" (Parravano 2014, 71). If one imagines how the American version of this picture book might look, it'd likely end with the boy snuggling between his parents in a monster-less bed, a clean conclusion that would communicate that parents can help. Problem solved.

Other examples of picture book imports from recent years that embrace ambiguities and, in some cases, untidy endings, include Stian Hole's *Anna's Heaven*, originally released in Norway and then in the United States in 2014; Wolf Erlbruch's *Duck, Death and the Tulip*, originally published in Germany in 2007 and then in 2011 in the States; and Avi Slodovnick's *The Tooth*, illustrated by Manon Gauthier and first published in Canada in 2009 (whose ending is certainly stark but also quite pensive). In 2008, German children saw Heinz Janisch's *The King and the Sea*, illustrated by Wolf Erlbruch, a collection of "21 Extremely Short Stories" involving a king who interacts with the likes of a bee, a tree, a ghost, a star, and a pencil. In one story, "The King and the Ghost," the king tells a ghost he doesn't believe in him. The ghost responds that he doesn't believe in kings. They agree one of them must be mistaken. And thus that short story concludes. The book will reach American readers in 2015, and it remains to be seen how they will respond to such an enigmatic book, a series of remarkably ambiguous, Zen-like stories.

Often, if we broaden what we're willing to read to children and expose them to picture book imports, we find the narrative rhythms of these imports are different. They are not what we are accustomed to with American picture books, especially when we look at recent Caldecott winners. There's a mismatch. It's almost as if we don't have a category for, say, Bárður Oskarsson's *The Flat Rabbit*, originally published in the Faroe Islands in 2011 but brought to the United States in 2014. In fact, Daniel Kraus in his *Booklist* review wrote: "Plenty of people are going to want nothing to do with this book." This dark story about how two characters deal with roadkill manages to be touching, while at the same time very open to interpretation. Oskarsson provides no answers, though as Kraus notes in his review, the book is a "very tactile wrestling with death that feels so honest" (Kraus 2014, unpaged). It's a book that crosses wires for many American readers. Caldecott winners, on the whole, like to wrap up stories and answer questions. The story itself might be clever or even bizarre (such as David Wiesner's *Mr. Wuffles!* or *Sector 7*), take us to strange and mysterious new worlds (Aaron Becker's *Journey*), embrace postmodernism (David Wiesner's groundbreaking *The Three Pigs*), make a point in subtle and ingenious ways (Laura Vaccaro Seeger's *Green*), and play with medium and style, even telling stories within stories (David Ezra Stein's *Interrupting Chicken*), but we are usually left with a feeling that the story is done.

Three possible exceptions are Barbara Lehman's *The Red Book*, a 2005 Caldecott Honor book, whose final page indicates that the story isn't over, as we see another child pick up the mysterious, enchanting red book of the title—much like the ending of David Wiesner's *Flotsam*, the 2007 Medal winner. Jon J Muth's 2006 Honor book, *Zen Shorts*, also embraces a certain amount of ambiguity in its narrative, given that it's a collection of stories from the teachings of the Buddha, and "'Zen shorts' are … ideas to puzzle over," Muth writes at the book's close. "They have no goal" (Muth 2005, unpaged).

But when looking at Caldecott winners from 2000 till today, the most striking exception seems to be Jon Klassen's *This Is Not My Hat*, the 2013 winner with no happily-ever-after for the protagonist, whose fate is left undetermined. Did he survive after the big fish retrieved the hat he'd stolen? Klassen leaves it a delicious mystery, just as he does the fate of the rabbit in 2011's *I Want My Hat Back*. In 2014, Mac Barnett's *Sam & Dave Dig a Hole*, a 2015 Caldecott Honor book, also illustrated by Klassen, delivered another entertaining and mysterious open ending. Klassen, who is originally from Canada, certainly seems to be changing the American picture book landscape with his willingness to let the story linger, instead of being wrapped up cleanly with a happy ending. In an interview on October 17, 2014, at the blog, *Art of the Picture Book*, Klassen addresses this: "When the premise suggests that this can end more ambiguously, and if there's more to be gained there, it should be allowed to do that," he said. "I think kids are fine with that. They can't necessarily tell you that they want sweeter things or edgier things. They just want a good story to be told as well as it can be told."

Perhaps it all comes down to a willingness on the part of those of other nationalities to embrace the questions themselves. Do Americans, on the whole and for whatever reason, prefer answers provided in our picture books? "It is very common to see European and Latin American picture books that raise more questions than they answer and don't come full-circle, tying up everything with a pretty bow," Bedrick of Enchanted Lion Books tells me, adding that she recently saw a "lovely little philosophical picture book" from Mexico about an animal who wants to know everything. "He reads books and asks big questions and has experiences in the world," she explains, "and the more of this he does, the better he understands that he cannot know everything and that there are so many questions that can't be answered. The end has him sitting there, pondering all of this, looking thoughtful, or vaguely sad (depending on how you read it), and I thought how lovely it was that he was sitting there musing in the face of the unanswerable, beset by mystery and the enduring questions. This felt like a very different book from what we see here, a beautiful book, a provocative book that we don't admit and make room for, because we need to conquer knowledge and what matters aren't the questions themselves but the answers" (Bedrick 2014b).

Indeed, picture book imports handle the subject of death in this manner as well, and we often see imports that face death, and other life challenges, head on. It seems that, more than with American picture books, those of other nationalities deem it "appropriate" for child readers to read about and ponder death and loss. To be sure, if we look at recent Caldecott winners, we do see characters coping with loss, for instance in Lane Smith's *Grandpa Green*, a 2012 Caldecott Honor book, as well as in Chris Raschka's *A Ball for Daisy*, the 2012 winner. But even in the end of the latter, the dog gets a new ball after grieving over the loss of the first. All's well that ends well. It's a beautiful book that fully deserves its many accolades, but when comparing it to imports, it shows us something about the closure American readers like to see.

If you compare it to the aforementioned picture books about death, such as Stian Hole's highly imaginative exploration of one girl's hard questions about her mother's death, you see more of a willingness to let the questions rest unanswered. In 2013, American readers saw Stein Erik Lunde's *My Father's Arms Are a Boat*, illustrated by Øyvind Torseter, which USBBY selected as a 2014 Outstanding International Book and which received a 2014 Batchelder Honor. Originally published in Norway in 2008, it was translated for the first American edition from Enchanted Lion Books. It's the story of a young boy whose mother has died. He and his father are trying to make some sense of the fresh grief inhabiting their home. It's a loss that readers ease into and discover slowly, a loss that Lunde and Torseter take on without flinching.

There are certainly Caldecott winners in the past decade that deal with loss and strife, but they tend to be historical fiction showing people overcoming issues related to class and/or politics. Peter Sís' *The Wall*, a 2008 Honor book; *Dave the Potter*, a 2011 Honor book written by Laban Carrick Hill and illustrated by Bryan Collier; and *Rosa*, a 2006 Honor book written by Nikki Giovanni and also illustrated by Bryan

Collier, are but a few examples. Many picture book imports are comfortable with showing conflicts of a more personal nature. Klaas Verplancke's *Applesauce*, originally released in Belgium in 2010, but in the United States two years later, is about a boy dealing with "thunder daddy" (Verplancke 2012, unpaged), whose mood changes on a dime, and in Pija Lindenbaum's Swedish import, *When Owen's Mom Breathed Fire* (on American shelves back in 2006), one young boy navigates his mother's strong moods and very bad day. Shaun Tan's *The Red Tree* (2001), originally published in Australia, addresses depression in an elegant, mysterious, and surreal manner. In one of the best imports in recent memory, Kyo Maclear's *Virginia Wolf*, illustrated by Isabelle Arsenault and originally published in Canada in 2012, the angry and quite possibly depressed protagonist is buoyed by her sister's efforts to cheer her.

On the whole, it's rare to see an American picture book dealing with loss, strife, or death in a way that doesn't attempt to provide answers or closure. Even in Molly Bang's 2000 Caldecott Honor book, *When Sophie Gets Angry—Really, Really Angry . . .*, where the protagonist addresses her fierce emotions on her own, the book's tidy ending notes, "Everything's back together again. And Sophie isn't angry anymore" (Bang 1999, unpaged). Two recent American picture books with striking open endings, one dealing with death and both dealing with power and bullying, are Bob Staake's *Bluebird* and Jacqueline Woodson's *Each Kindness*, illustrated by E. B. Lewis. These are two books that were discussed and praised at the *Horn Book*'s blog, *Calling Caldecott*, yet neither one was named a Medal or Honor book.

Bedrick explains one possible reason for these differences. "In many countries," she tells me, "children still read picture books up to the age of ten or so. These books are not being written and published just for the youngest children. So the content of picture books tends to be broader and deeper in countries where eight- to ten-year-olds are still actively engaged in reading them. Here in the United States, children are pushed out of picture books at such a young age that more sophisticated and evolved content is often seen to be inappropriate for the picture book format." She also adds that other cultures are less cut off from death than we are and tells the story of marveling to an editor in Mexico about the frequency of death and loss in their books. The editor's response to Claudia was that in Mexico death and life are part of the same thing (Bedrick 2014b).

As someone who believes in the value of imports, I hope to see more offerings from certain countries whose books we simply don't see often here in America. "I'm on the lookout for African artists, because I love Africa's rich visual tradition" (Mouly 2014), says Françoise Mouly, publisher and editorial director of TOON Books. "It is true that we just aren't seeing enough books from Africa being published in North America. I would love to have more on our list" (Barry 2014), adds Sheila Barry from Groundwood, who says they are also working to translate more books from Arabic. "Not all countries are as richly represented online as others," Bedrick explains. "African books are harder to find than those from Scandinavian countries. Arab [ones are] hard to find. Even a lot of Japanese material isn't in English online. If an editor works like a hunter," she adds, "there's a lot to be found" (Bedrick 2014b). Says Alex

Spiro, cofounder and creative director of Flying Eye Books, "The Latin American contingent appears to be growing steadily, and there is some fantastic new work coming out of Brazil, as well as Mexico" (Spiro 2014). As for India, it's relatively easy for American readers to read some of their offerings, thanks to Tara Books.

Spiro adds that there is an abundance of groundbreaking work on the international scene that doesn't make it into the English language markets "for fear of some incompatibility with local yarn-spinning tastes" (Spiro 2014). I, for one, hope that changes, since good stories are universal and there is great art to be seen the world over. And there's no doubt that bringing imports to American children is well worth the effort. Liz Bicknell, executive vice president, associate publisher, and editorial director of Candlewick Press, sums it up well: "If the complexities of language barriers, distance, and time zones can be overcome, it's rewarding to feel you are bringing something different to American children" (Bicknell 2014).

References

Art of the Picture Book. www.artofthepicturebook.com/-check-in-with/2014/10/15/interview
  -with-jon-klassen.

Bang, Molly. 1999. *When Sophie Gets Angry—Really, Really Angry . . .* New York: Scholastic.

Barry, Sheila. 2014. E-mail message to author. December 4.

Bedrick, Claudia Zoe. 2014a. "2014 Batchelder Award Acceptance Speech." *American Library Association Institutional Repository.* June 30. https://alair.ala.org/handle/11213/305.

Bedrick, Claudia Zoe. 2014b. E-mail message to author. December 14 and 15.

Bicknell, Liz. 2014. E-mail message to author. December 7 and January 6, 2015.

Kraus, Daniel. 2014. Review of *The Flat Rabbit*, by Bárður Oskarsson. *Booklist Online.* www.booklistonline.com/The-Flat-Rabbit-Bardur-Oskarsson/pid=6867161.

Lennon, Heather. 2014. E-mail message to author. November 25.

Liniers. 2014. *What There Is Before There Is Anything There: A Scary Story.* Translated by Elisa Amado. Toronto: Groundwood Books.

Mouly, Françoise. 2014. E-mail message to author. December 5.

Muth, Jon J 2005. *Zen Shorts.* New York: Scholastic.

Neugebauer, Michael. 2014. E-mail message to author. December 1.

Parravano, Martha V. 2014. Review of *What There Is Before There Is Anything There: A Scary Story*, by Liniers. *The Horn Book* XC (6): 71.

Spiro, Alex. 2014. E-mail message to author. December 2.

Verplancke, Klaas. 2012. *Applesauce.* Translated by Helen Mixter. Toronto: Groundwood Books.

The
Newbery
Awards

2015–1922

2015 Newbery Award

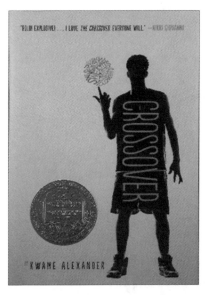

The Crossover

By Kwame Alexander

HOUGHTON MIFFLIN HARCOURT

Twelve-year-old narrator Josh Bell uses the rhythms of a poetry jam to emulate the "moving & grooving/popping and rocking" of life on the basketball court with his twin brother, J.B. This powerful novel in verse paints an authentic portrait of a closely-knit family on the brink of crisis. Swish! This book is nothing but net!

"Our 15-member committee worked diligently and thoughtfully to determine the 2015 Newbery Medal winner," said Committee Chair Randall Enos.

ABOUT THE AUTHOR

Kwame Alexander is a poet and author of 18 books, including *Acoustic Rooster and His Barnyard Band* and *He Said, She Said*. He is founder of Book-in-a-Day, a student-run publishing program that has created more than 3,000 student authors; and LEAP for Ghana, an international literacy project that builds libraries, trains teachers, and empowers children through literature. He visits schools and libraries, has owned several publishing companies, written for stage and television, and taught high school. In 2015, Alexander will serve as Bank Street College of Education's first writer-in-residence.

PHOTOGRAPH BY NATAKI HEWLING

2015 NEWBERY HONOR BOOKS

El Deafo
By Cece Bell
AMULET BOOKS/ABRAMS

In this insightful and humorous graphic novel memoir, Cece Bell portrays growing up with a giant hearing aid strapped to her chest. Themes of navigating a new school, sleepovers, finding a true friend, and a first crush make this book universal in appeal. Bell shows that our differences are gifts that "can be turned into something amazing."

Brown Girl Dreaming
By Jacqueline Woodson
PENGUIN/NANCY PAULSEN BOOKS

Jacqueline Woodson's lyrical memoir chronicles the incidents and emotions she experienced as an African American girl growing up in the 1960s and 1970s. Precise language magnifies moments and connects them to the larger historical narrative. Her elegant and evocative standalone poems weave a story about her development from a struggling reader and dreamer into a confident young woman and writer.

2014 AWARD

Flora & Ulysses: The Illuminated Adventures by Kate DiCamillo, illustrated by K. G. Campbell. CANDLEWICK.

Comic book fan and natural-born cynic Flora Belle Buckman and Ulysses, a flying, superhero, squirrel, join forces to overcome Ulysses's arch-nemesis, Flora's mother, and encounter a quirky cast of characters in this homage to comic books.

HONORS

Doll Bones by Holly Black. MARGARET K. McELDERRY BOOKS, AN IMPRINT OF SIMON & SCHUSTER CHILDREN'S PUBLISHING DIVISION.

Best friends Zach, Poppy, and Alice set out on a life-altering quest driven by the presence of a sinister bone china doll who haunts their dreams and waking hours.

The Year of Billy Miller by Kevin Henkes, GREENWILLOW BOOKS. AN IMPRINT OF HARPERCOLLINS PUBLISHERS.

Billy Miller starts second grade with a bump on his head and a lot of worries, but during the year he develops better relationships with his teacher, his little sister, and his parents, and celebrates a quiet triumph of his own.

One Came Home by Amy Timberlake, ALFRED A. KNOPF, AN IMPRINT OF RANDOM HOUSE CHILDREN'S BOOKS, A DIVISION OF RANDOM HOUSE, INC.

In 1871 Wisconsin, love, betrayal, grief, and violence spur 13-year-old Georgie on a gripping adventure full of hardship, heartbreak, and terror, as she tries to solve the mystery of her sister's disappearance.

Paperboy by Vince Vawter, DELACORTE PRESS, AN IMPRINT OF RANDOM HOUSE CHILDREN'S BOOKS, A DIVISION OF RANDOM HOUSE, INC.

A sensitive and resilient boy who stutters, ventures beyond the familiar and finds his voice while taking over his best friend's paper route. Set in the summer of 1959 Memphis, *Paperboy* is a moving coming-of-age novel.

2013 AWARD

The One and Only Ivan by Katherine Applegate, illustrated by Patricia Castelao. HARPERCOLLINS CHILDREN'S BOOKS, A DIVISION OF HARPERCOLLINS PUBLISHERS.

Ivan's transformative emergence from the "Ape at Exit 8" to "The One and Only Ivan, Mighty Silverback," comes to life through the gorilla's own distinct narrative voice, filled with wry humor, deep emotion, and insights into the nature of friendship, hope, and humanity.

HONORS

Splendors and Glooms by Laura Amy Schlitz. CANDLEWICK.

Lizzie Rose, Parsefall, and Clara are caught in the clutches of a wicked puppeteer and a powerful witch in this deliciously dark and complex tale set in Dickensian England.

Bomb: The Race to Build—and Steal—the World's Most Dangerous Weapon by Steve Sheinkin. FLASH POINT, AN IMPRINT OF ROARING BROOK PRESS.

Balancing intersecting threads of scientific discovery, political intrigue, and military strategy, "Bomb" is a riveting historical nonfiction drama about the creation of the ultimate weapon.

Three Times Lucky **by Sheila Turnage. DIAL BOOKS FOR YOUNG READERS, A DIVISION OF PENGUIN YOUNG READERS GROUP.**

In the rich tradition of Southern storytelling, Mo LoBeau leads the eccentric residents of Tupelo Landing, North Carolina, on a rollicking journey of mystery, adventure, and small-town intrigue as she investigates a murder and searches for her long-lost mother.

2012 AWARD

Dead End in Norvelt **by Jack Gantos. FARRAR, STRAUS AND GIROUX.**

The importance of history and reading (so you don't do the same "stupid stuff" again) is at the heart of this achingly funny romp through a dying New Deal town. While mopping up epic nose bleeds, Jack narrates this screw-ball mystery in an endearing and believable voice.

HONORS

Inside Out & Back Again **by Thanhha Lai. HARPERCOLLINS CHILDREN'S BOOKS. A DIVISION OF HARPERCOLLINS PUBLISHERS.**

Hà and her family flee war-torn Vietnam for the American South. In spare, vivid verse, she chronicles her struggle to find her place in a new and shifting world.

Breaking Stalin's Nose **by Eugene Yelchin, illustrated by the author. HENRY HOLT AND COMPANY, LLC.**

On the eve of his induction into the Young Pioneers, Sasha's world is overturned when his father is arrested by Stalin's guard. Yelchin deftly crafts a stark and compelling story of a child's lost idealism.

2011 AWARD

Moon over Manifest **by Clare Vanderpool. DELACORTE PRESS, AN IMPRINT OF RANDOM HOUSE CHILDREN'S BOOKS.**

This big-hearted, multigenerational epic set in small-town Kansas alternates between World War I and the Great Depression, but never strays too far from the tough-yet-vulnerable heroine, Abilene Tucker. With a mix of letters, newspaper articles, and a fortune teller's tales, the eclectic people and mysteries of Manifest spring to life.

HONORS

Turtle in Paradise by **Jennifer L. Holm**. RANDOM HOUSE CHILDREN'S BOOKS, A DIVISION OF RANDOM HOUSE, INC.

Sassy eleven-year-old Turtle finds her life turned on end when she is sent to live with her aunt in Depression-era Key West. With vivid details, witty dialogue, and outrageous escapades, Holm successfully explores the meaning of family and home . . . and lost treasures found.

Heart of a Samurai by **Margi Preus**. AMULET BOOKS, AN IMPRINT OF ABRAMS.

Shipwrecks, whaling, a search for home, and a delightful exploration of cultures create a swashbuckling adventure. This historical novel is based on the true story of Manjiro (later John Mung), the young fisherman believed to be the first Japanese person to visit America who, against all odds, became a Samurai.

Dark Emperor and Other Poems of the Night by **Joyce Sidman** / Illustrated by **Rick Allen**. HOUGHTON MIFFLIN BOOKS FOR CHILDREN, HOUGHTON MIFFLIN HARCOURT.

Welcoming her readers into the "wild, enchanted park" that is the night, Sidman has elegantly crafted twelve poems rich in content and varied in form. Companion prose pieces about nocturnal flora and fauna are as tuneful and graceful as the poems.

One Crazy Summer by **Rita Williams-Garcia**. AMISTAD, AN IMPRINT OF HARPERCOLLINS PUBLISHERS.

The voices of sisters Delphine, Vonetta, and Fern sing in three-part harmony in this wonderfully nuanced, humorous novel set in 1968 Oakland, California. One crazy summer, the three girls find adventure when they are sent to meet their estranged poet-mother Cecile, who prints flyers for the Black Panthers.

2010 AWARD

When You Reach Me by **Rebecca Stead**. WENDY LAMB BOOKS, AN IMPRINT OF RANDOM HOUSE CHILDREN'S BOOKS.

Twelve-year-old Miranda encounters shifting friendships, a sudden punch, a strange homeless man, and mysterious notes that hint at knowledge of the future. These and other seemingly random events converge in a brilliantly constructed plot.

HONORS

Claudette Colvin: Twice Toward Justice by **Phillip Hoose**. MELANIE KROUPA BOOKS/FARRAR STRAUS GIROUX.

Hoose reveals the true story of an unsung hero of the Montgomery bus boycott in a work that seamlessly merges Colvin's own recollections with the narrative voice, providing a uniquely personal view of Colvin and the civil rights movement.

The Evolution of Calpurnia Tate by Jacqueline Kelly. HENRY HOLT BOOKS FOR YOUNG READERS.

On the eve of the twentieth century, eleven-year-old Calpurnia awakens to new possibilities and, through her evolving relationship with her naturalist grandfather, learns to think like a scientist.

Where the Mountain Meets the Moon by Grace Lin. LITTLE, BROWN BOOKS FOR YOUNG READERS.

A rich tapestry of stories, both original and traditional, transports readers to a fantastic world where Dragon joins Minli on a fortune-changing quest.

The Mostly True Adventures of Homer P. Figg by Rodman Philbrick. THE BLUE SKY PRESS, AN IMPRINT OF SCHOLASTIC INC.

This rollicking yarn, presented through the voice of twelve-year-old Homer, uses humor and pluck to mitigate the horrors of the Civil War.

2009 AWARD

The Graveyard Book by Neil Gaiman, illustrated by Dave McKean. HARPERCOLLINS.

A delicious mix of murder, fantasy, humor, and human longing, the tale of Nobody Owens is told in magical, haunting prose. A child marked for death by an ancient league of assassins escapes into an abandoned graveyard, where he is reared and protected by its spirit denizens.

HONORS

The Underneath by Kathi Appelt, illustrated by David Small. ATHENEUM.

Intertwining stories of an embittered man, a loyal hound, an abandoned cat, and a vengeful lamia sing of love, loss, loneliness, and hope.

The Surrender Tree: Poems of Cuba's Struggle for Freedom by Margarita Engle. HENRY HOLT.

Compelling free verse in alternating voices lyrically tells the story of Cuba's three wars for independence from Spain. Combining real-life characters (such as legendary healer Rosa La Bayamesa) with imagined individuals, Engle focuses on Rosa's struggle to save everyone—black or white, Cuban or Spanish, friend or enemy.

Savvy by Ingrid Law. DIAL.

This rich first-person narrative draws readers into a wild bus ride, winding through the countryside on a journey of self-discovery for Mibs Beaumont and her companions.

After Tupac & D Foster by Jacqueline Woodson. PUTNAM.

This tightly woven novel looks back on two years in a New York City neighborhood, where life changes for two eleven-year-olds when a new girl joins their game of double Dutch.

2008 AWARD

Good Masters! Sweet Ladies! Voices from a Medieval Village by Laura Amy Schlitz, illustrated by Robert Byrd. CANDLEWICK.

Thirteenth-century England springs to life in twenty-one dramatic individual narratives that introduce young inhabitants of village and manor, from Hugo, the lord's nephew, to Nelly, the sniggler. Schlitz's elegant monologues and dialogues draw back the curtain on the period, revealing character and relationships and hinting at stories untold.

HONORS

Elijah of Buxton by Christopher Paul Curtis. SCHOLASTIC.

Elijah is the first free-born child in Buxton, a Canadian community of escaped slaves, in 1860. With masterful storytelling, vibrant humor, and poignant insight into the realities of slavery and the meaning of freedom, Curtis takes readers on a journey that transforms a "fragile" eleven-year-old boy into a courageous hero.

The Wednesday Wars by Gary D. Schmidt. CLARION.

Seventh-grader Holling Hoodhood is convinced his teacher hates him. Through their Wednesday afternoon Shakespeare sessions she helps him cope with events both wildly funny and deadly serious. "To thine own self be true" is just one of the life lessons he learns.

Feathers by Jacqueline Woodson. PUTNAM.

A new boy's arrival in a sixth-grade classroom helps Frannie recognize the barriers that separate people and the importance of hope as a bridge. Transcendent imagery and lyrical prose deftly capture a girl learning to navigate the world through words.

2007 AWARD

The Higher Power of Lucky by Susan Patron, illustrated by Matt Phelan. RICHARD JACKSON/ATHENEUM.

Patron takes readers to the California desert community of Hard Pan (population 43), where ten-year-old Lucky Trimble eavesdrops on twelve-step program meetings from her hiding place behind Hard Pan's Found Object Wind Chime Museum &

Visitor Center. Eccentric characters and quirky details spice up Lucky's life just as fresh parsley embellishes her guardian Brigitte's French cuisine.

HONORS

Penny from Heaven by Jennifer L. Holm. RANDOM HOUSE.

Eleven-year-old Penny looks forward to spending the summer rooting for the Brooklyn Dodgers and scheming with her cousin Frankie. Instead she navigates the space between her two families and uncovers the reason for their estrangement in this funny and touching tale of intergenerational love set in 1953.

Hattie Big Sky by Kirby Larson. DELACORTE.

Sixteen-year-old orphan Hattie Brooks is looking for a place to belong—a home. In 1918 she leaves Iowa for the Montana prairie. In this engaging first-person narrative, Hattie strives to forge a new life. Vivid imagery and careful attention to historical detail distinguish this memorable novel that portrays her struggle to "prove her claim."

Rules by Cynthia Lord. SCHOLASTIC.

"A boy can take off his shirt to swim, but not his shorts." Twelve-year-old Catherine creates rules for her younger, autistic brother David in an attempt to normalize his life and her own. In her debut novel, Lord's heroine learns to use words to forge connections with her brother, her workaholic father, and a paraplegic friend.

2006 AWARD

Criss Cross by Lynne Rae Perkins. GREENWILLOW.

Criss Cross follows the lives of four fourteen-year-olds in a small town. Each at their own crossroads, this ensemble cast explores new thoughts and feelings in their quest to find the meaning of life and love. In thirty-eight brief chapters, this poetic, postmodern novel experiments with a variety of styles: haiku, song lyrics, question-and-answer dialogue, and split-screen scenarios.

HONORS

Whittington by Alan Armstrong, illustrated by S. D. Schindler. RANDOM HOUSE.

Armstrong creates a glorious barnyard fantasy that seamlessly weaves together three tales: Whittington the cat's arrival on Bernie's farm, his retelling of the traditional legend of his fourteenth-century namesake, and one boy's struggle to learn to read. The tales unite the disparate citizens of the barn community in a celebration of oral and written language, the support of friends, the healing power of humor, and the triumph of life.

Hitler Youth: Growing Up in Hitler's Shadow by **Susan Campbell Bartoletti.**
SCHOLASTIC.

How could the Holocaust have happened? Bartoletti delivers a chilling answer by
exploring Hitler's rise to power through the firsthand experiences of young followers
whose adolescent zeal he so successfully exploited and the more extraordinary few who
risked certain death in resisting. The meticulously researched volume traces the Hitler
Youth movement from the early 1930s through the defeat of the Third Reich.

Princess Academy by **Shannon Hale. BLOOMSBURY CHILDREN'S BOOKS.**

Miri and the other young women of her rocky highland village are forced to leave
their close-knit community when the prince must choose a bride. Miri soon becomes
the strong, resilient, and courageous leader of the academy. The book is a fresh
approach to the traditional princess story with unexpected plot twists and great emotional resonance.

Show Way by **Jacqueline Woodson, illustrated by Hudson Talbott. PUTNAM.**

Jacqueline Woodson's magnificent poem "Show Way" tells the story of slavery, eman-
cipation, and triumph for each generation of her maternal ancestors. She pays tribute
to the creative women who guided their "tall and straight-boned" daughters to courage, self-sufficiency, and freedom. Whether with quilts or stories, poems or songs,
these women discovered and shared the strength to carry on.

2005 AWARD

Kira-Kira by **Cynthia Kadohata. ATHENEUM.**

Two sisters lie on their backs, watching the stars and repeating the Japanese word for
"glittering"—"kira-kira." Like this quiet opening scene, Kadohata's tenderly nuanced
novel glitters with plain and poignant words that describe the strong love within a
Japanese American family from the point of view of younger sister Katie. Personal
challenges and family tragedy are set against the oppressive social climate of the
South during the 1950s and early 1960s.

HONORS

Al Capone Does My Shirts by **Gennifer Choldenko. PUTNAM.**

With Alcatraz as the evocative backdrop for this highly original novel set in 1935,
twelve-year-old Moose Flanagan tells about the travails of "the Rock," where his
father has taken a job. Hilarious antics are deftly interwoven with themes of isolation
and imprisonment, compassion and connection.

The Voice That Challenged a Nation: Marian Anderson and the Struggle for Equal Rights by **Russell Freedman**. CLARION.

The Voice That Challenged a Nation meticulously explores resonant themes with the masterful structure of a musical composition. Eloquent, economic prose sheds a personal light on one woman's sometimes reluctant role as a symbol in the struggle against racism and her calling to share an illustrious gift.

Lizzie Bright and the Buckminster Boy by **Gary D. Schmidt**. CLARION.

Set in Maine in 1912 and propelled by a tragic historical event, Schmidt's powerfully haunting novel probes a forbidden friendship between a preacher's son and a dark-skinned girl from a nearby island. Steeped in imagery and laced with surprising humor, Lizzie Bright and the Buckminster Boy explores powerlessness, possibility, and the profound impact individuals can make.

2004 AWARD

The Tale of Despereaux: Being the Story of a Mouse, a Princess, Some Soup, and a Spool of Thread by **Kate DiCamillo, illustrated by Timothy Basil Ering**. CANDLEWICK.

The Tale of Despereaux draws the reader into an enchanting account of a smaller-than-usual mouse in love with music, stories, and a princess named Pea. With character and plot far more complex than the traditional fairy tale, separate stories introduce Despereaux, condemned for talking to the princess; the evil rat, Roscuro, who loves light and soup; and Miggery Sow, a farm girl with royal aspirations. Their fates are threaded together as Despereaux undertakes a hero's quest that culminates in mice, rats, and humans living almost happily ever after.

HONORS

Olive's Ocean by **Kevin Henkes**. GREENWILLOW.

Twelve-year-old Martha receives a page from the journal of a classmate, Olive, who has died in an accident. Olive's entry about a desire to be Martha's friend, to see the ocean, and to become a writer propels Martha into a journey from childhood to the brink of adolescence.

An American Plague: The True and Terrifying Story of the Yellow Fever Epidemic of 1793 by **Jim Murphy**. CLARION.

An American Plague: The True and Terrifying Story of the Yellow Fever Epidemic of 1793 dramatically recounts the story of the yellow fever epidemic that nearly decimated the population of Philadelphia at the end of the eighteenth century. Integrating newspapers, diaries, personal testimonies, and period illustrations, the narrative delivers a social and medical history of the times and raises chilling questions about the disease today.

2003 AWARD

Crispin: The Cross of Lead **by Avi. HYPERION.**

Crispin: The Cross of Lead is an action-filled page-turner set in fourteenth-century England. "Asta's son" is the only name the thirteen-year-old title character has ever known when he is suddenly orphaned and stripped of home and possessions. Accused of murder and wanted dead or alive, Crispin flees his village and falls in with a juggler, Bear, who becomes his protector and teacher. Relentlessly pursued by Crispin's enemies, the pair flees to solve the mystery of his identity and fight the injustices of feudalism.

HONORS

The House of the Scorpion **by Nancy Farmer. RICHARD JACKSON/ATHENEUM.**

Farmer tackles the provocative topics of cloning, the value of life, illegal immigration, and the drug trade in a coming-of-age novel set in a desolate, futuristic desert.

Pictures of Hollis Woods **by Patricia Reilly Giff. RANDOM HOUSE.**

Twelve-year-old Hollis Woods unfolds her story of foster care and a search for family in images from her sketchbook, which reveal both her memories and her artistic soul. Strong visual imagery, multi-layered structure, and memorable characters create an emotionally satisfying story.

Hoot **by Carl Hiaasen. KNOPF.**

Hiaasen's wildly funny satire features the new kid, Roy, joining forces with tough Beatrice and the elusive Mullet Fingers to defeat a bully, thwart an avaricious corporation, and save a colony of burrowing owls. Hiaasen's work is both a rollicking adventure and a serious examination of values that threaten our environment.

A Corner of the Universe **by Ann M. Martin. SCHOLASTIC.**

With the surprising arrival of a mentally disabled uncle, twelve-year-old Hattie Owen's world is turned upside down. Ann Martin used her own childhood memories to create a 1960s small-town setting, perfectly suited to this poignant story.

Surviving the Applewhites **by Stephanie S. Tolan. HARPERCOLLINS.**

Tolan features pierced and spike-haired Jake, who has been expelled from every possible public school before his unwilling arrival at Wit's End, N.C., and the home-school run by the chaotic and outrageous Applewhite family. The eccentric characters and fast pace culminate in a hilarious musical production that forces Jake to grow.

2002 AWARD

A Single Shard by **Linda Sue Park**. CLARION.

Park takes readers to twelfth-century Korea to tell a timeless story of dedication to one's dreams and art in *A Single Shard*. Tree-ear, an orphan, becomes fascinated with a nearby community of potters. Drawn by their exquisite craftsmanship, the adolescent boy begins to assist the master potter Min. Tree-ear's determination and bravery in pursuing his dream of becoming a potter take readers on a literary journey that demonstrates how courage, honor, and perseverance can overcome great odds and bring great happiness.

HONORS

Everything on a Waffle by **Polly Horvath**. FARRAR STRAUS GIROUX.

When eleven-year-old Primrose Squarp's parents disappear at sea, her faith in their return defies all adult logic. Set in British Columbia, *Everything on a Waffle* combines quirky characters, recipes, and amazing twists of plot in a striking combination of the barely credible and profoundly true.

Carver: A Life in Poems by **Marilyn Nelson**. FRONT STREET.

Nelson challenges readers with a truly new biography of George Washington Carver. Told from multiple perspectives, this collection of fifty-nine poems reveals little-known facets of the remarkable scientist, who it too often dismissed as "the peanut man." With simple sophistication and beauty, Nelson transcends Carver's brilliance and scientific achievements to present the essence of this profoundly humble man.

2001 AWARD

A Year Down Yonder by **Richard Peck**. DIAL.

A linked series of vignettes set in rural Illinois during the Depression, *A Year Down Yonder* tells the story of fifteen-year-old Mary Alice who leaves Chicago to spend a year with Grandma Dowdel. Her initial apprehension about life in a small town with a scheming old woman gradually gives way to admiration and love as she recognizes the warm heart behind Grandma's shenanigans.

HONORS

Hope Was Here by **Joan Bauer**. PUTNAM.

Hope Was Here relates how sixteen-year-old Hope and her aunt move to a small town in Wisconsin to join the "short order dance" of life at the Welcome Stairways Diner. In the course of just a few months, Hope encounters issues as diverse as her customers: corruption in politics, a new love, serious illness, and the meaning of family.

The Wanderer by Sharon Creech. JOANNA COTLER/HARPERCOLLINS.

Sailing across the Atlantic with her uncles and cousins becomes a journey of discovery for thirteen-year-old Sophie. The carefully designed plot gradually reveals the truth of Sophie's past, even as readers begin to wonder about this rag-tag crew. Through journal entries, multiple viewpoints are weaved into a story that speaks to the power of survival and the delicacy of grief.

Because of Winn-Dixie by Kate DiCamillo. CANDLEWICK.

When a stray dog appears almost magically in the midst of the produce section of the Winn-Dixie grocery store, he leads ten-year-old India Opal Buloni from one new friend to the next in a small Florida town. The stories she hears from each one help her to piece together a new definition of family.

Joey Pigza Loses Control by Jack Gantos. FARRAR STRAUS GIROUX.

Spending the summer with his estranged father, Joey longs for the two of them to be winners together, but their lives gradually spiral out of control. As the old "wired" Joey returns, readers will long to see him regain his balance in an out-of-kilter world. Like many family stories, this is a tale whose pain is generously laced with humor.

2000 AWARD

Bud, Not Buddy by Christopher Paul Curtis. DELACORTE.

Ten-year-old Bud Caldwell runs away from a foster home and begins an unforgettable journey in search of his father. His only clues are old flyers left by his now-deceased mother that point to a legendary jazz bandleader. Bud's fast-paced first-person account moves with the rhythms of jazz and celebrates life, family, and a child's indomitable spirit.

HONORS

Getting Near to Baby by Audrey Couloumbis. PUTNAM.

Twelve-year-old Willa Jo and Little Sister, whose voice is "lost in sadness," live with bossy Aunt Patty following the death of their baby sister. Willa Jo finds haven on the roof and from sunrise to sunset recalls recent events and helps her family come to terms with its tragedy.

26 Fairmount Avenue by Tomie dePaola, illustrated by the author. PUTNAM.

DePaola looks back to 1938 when his family, overcoming fire and flood, builds a new house. That year Tomie "quits" kindergarten, shares "chocolates" with Nana upstairs, critiques a movie, practices mural art, and finally moves to 26 Fairmount Avenue.

Our Only May Amelia by Jennifer L. Holm. HARPERCOLLINS.

Growing up as the only girl in a large Finnish-American farming family along Washington's Nasel River in 1899, 12-year-old May Amelia prefers tricks and adventures to being a "proper young lady." Unjustly blamed for tragedy, May must leave home before returning to claim her rightful place.

1999 AWARD

Holes by Louis Sachar. FRANCES FOSTER/FARRAR STRAUS GIROUX.

Stanley Yelnats, the heir to his family's curse of bad luck, is convicted of a crime he didn't commit. He serves his sentence at Camp Green Lake, a dry, flat wasteland where the warden assigns each inmate the task of digging one hole every day. Hole by hole, Stanley and his friend Zero dig their destiny.

Published in a new edition with bonus material in 2008 (Farrar Straus Giroux).

HONOR

A Long Way from Chicago: A Novel in Stories by Richard Peck. DIAL.

An old man looks back on rollicking summers spent with his larger-than-life grandmother during the Great Depression in this colorful novel made up of seven masterfully interwoven tales.

1998 AWARD

Out of the Dust by Karen Hesse. SCHOLASTIC.

Fourteen-year-old Billie Jo relates how her mother dies after an accident with burning kerosene. Blaming both herself and her father, she is unable to express herself through her piano playing because of the burns that scar her hands. She leaves but quickly returns to her home "of dust" and she realizes how much a part of her it is.

HONORS

Lily's Crossing by Patricia Reilly Giff. DELACORTE.

During her 1944 summer vacation in the Rockaways, ten-year-old Lily's best friend moves away and her beloved father Poppy goes off to war. Then Lily meets Albert, a young Hungarian refugee with whom she builds a poignant friendship based on shared loneliness, secrets, and lies.

Ella Enchanted by Gail Carson Levine. HARPERCOLLINS.

Spunky, stubborn, and very clever, this new Cinderella spends a lifetime trying to outwit the curse of a fairy's unwelcome gift of obedience. In a kingdom populated with ogres, giants, princes, and fairies, Ella begins a fruitless quest to have the curse lifted, only to discover that she has that power within herself.

Wringer by Jerry Spinelli. JOANNA COTLER/HARPERCOLLINS.

Palmer LaRue dreads his approaching birthday because he does not want to be a wringer, one of the ten-year-old boys who breaks the necks of pigeons wounded at the town's pigeon shoot fund-raiser. When his three bullying friends suspect he is sheltering a stray pigeon, Palmer decides to take a personal stand against this annual rite of passage.

1997 AWARD

The View from Saturday by E. L. Konigsburg. JEAN KARL/ATHENEUM.

Mrs. Olinski selects four of her sixth-grade students to be the Academic Bowl team. No one understands her choice of these particular students, including Mrs. Olinski, who continues to question herself. The students surprise everyone with their unique contributions to the challenges of competition.

HONORS

A Girl Named Disaster by Nancy Farmer. ORCHARD.

When Nhamo (Disaster) flees her village to search for her father in Zimbabwe, she is lost on Lake Cabora Bassa in Mozambique. Alone, she survives harsh weather, wild animals, and near starvation before building a new life in the world of her father's people.

Moorchild by Eloise McGraw. MARGARET K. MCELDERRY BOOKS.

Moorchild Moql becomes the changeling Saaski, half-human, half-Folk, and an outcast in both worlds. The reader is drawn into the lives of the moorfolk who fear Saaski and those who try to understand her and support her.

The Thief by Megan Whalen Turner. GREENWILLOW.

Freed from the royal dungeons and commanded to steal an ancient talisman from supernatural guardians, young Gen pulls off an astonishing scam and in the process rescues his own country from a threatened invasion.

Belle Prater's Boy by Ruth White. FARRAR STRAUS GIROUX.

Gypsy's cousin Woodrow comes to live next door, bringing with him a mystery and the key to a secret that Gypsy keeps from herself. Grandparents and Gypsy's supportive mother and stepfather create a loving environment in which the children can come to grips with their losses.

1996 AWARD

The Midwife's Apprentice by **Karen Cushman**. CLARION.

The central character, Brat, is a homeless waif who first appears sleeping in a dung heap "unwashed, unnourished, unloved, and unlovely. . . ." From a person with no hopes, no dreams, and no expectations she becomes the midwife's apprentice—a person with a name and a place in the world. An excellent portrayal of medieval England.

HONORS

What Jamie Saw by **Carolyn Coman**. FRONT STREET.

What Jamie Saw is a gripping interior novel that portrays a desperate mother and her quietly heroic son as they move from an impossibly bleak situation toward a promise of hope. Coman captures Jamie's fear, his uncertainty, and his confusion as well as his growing confidence and ability to stand up for himself.

The Watsons Go to Birmingham—1963 by **Christopher Paul Curtis**. DELACORTE.

From its hilarious opening chapters to its shattering conclusion, *The Watsons Go to Birmingham* is a compelling novel that brings to life an African-American family. It draws together everyday events in such a way as to send the Watsons on a journey to Birmingham that will change them forever. The depiction of devastating events in Birmingham integrates the dichotomy of familial love and stability with the racial strife of the 1960s.

Yolonda's Genius by **Carol Fenner**. MARGARET K. MCELDERRY BOOKS.

Fenner portrays memorable characters and a vivid, authentic place in this engaging story of a bright, feisty fifth grader. Yolonda is determined to bring to light her younger brother's extraordinary talent of transforming the world around him into the music he makes.

The Great Fire by **Jim Murphy**. SCHOLASTIC.

The riveting narrative of the 1871 Chicago fire thrusts the reader into the center of the raging conflagration. Murphy weaves eyewitness accounts of the disaster with factual and social commentary, period photographs, etchings, and maps into memorable nonfiction writing.

1995 AWARD

Walk Two Moons by **Sharon Creech**. HARPERCOLLINS.

Thirteen-year-old Salamanca Tree Hiddle sets out on a cross-country journey with her grandparents to see her mother, who has not returned from a visit to Idaho. Sal entertains her grandparents by telling them about her new friend Phoebe, and in so doing begins to understand herself and her own mother. The book, packed with humor and affection, is an odyssey of unexpected twists and surprising conclusions.

HONORS

Catherine, Called Birdy by Karen Cushman. CLARION.

In the course of her fourteenth year, Catherine keeps a journal of her perceptive observations and longings for adventure and independence. Her lively, humorous descriptions of life on a thirteenth-century English manor, amid unwanted suitors and ever-present fleas, reach through time to speak to modern readers.

The Ear, the Eye, and the Arm by Nancy Farmer. ORCHARD.

A kidnapping of the General's three children in twenty-second-century Zimbabwe sets off a dramatic chase. In a series of extraordinary adventures, the children play a crucial role in a thrilling battle against the forces of evil. This futuristic detective story is interwoven with Africa's history, present-day concerns, and a variety of colorful characters.

1994 AWARD

The Giver by Lois Lowry. HOUGHTON MIFFLIN.

Twelve-year-old Jonas performs well in the impressively ordered society that the Elders have developed. But when he is selected to be the new "Receiver," Jonas begins to unravel the truth that underlies his world.

HONORS

Crazy Lady! by Jane Leslie Conly. LAURA GERINGER/HARPERCOLLINS.

Twelve-year-old Vernon's initially reluctant, off-beat friendship with an alcoholic and her developmentally disabled son has repercussions throughout the neighborhood, changing the lives of all involved. The reader becomes aware that Vernon's growing self-esteem and maturity come about through his commitment to helping his friends.

Eleanor Roosevelt: A Life of Discovery by Russell Freedman. CLARION.

Through compelling text and contemporary photographs, Eleanor Roosevelt is shown moving from a sheltered, unhappy childhood to the world's stage. This fascinating biography of a remarkable and complex woman is meticulously researched.

Dragon's Gate by Laurence Yep. HARPERCOLLINS.

Dragon's Gate is a carefully researched, well-written account of the lives of the Chinese who built the transcontinental railroad in the Sierra Mountains. This glimpse into the complex working community of California at the time of the Civil War is also a sensitive portrayal of the relationship between a father and son.

1993 AWARD

Missing May by **Cynthia Rylant. ORCHARD.**

Twelve-year-old Summer lives with her Aunt May and Uncle Ob in the mountains of West Virginia. When May dies, Summer, Uncle Ob, and Summer's friend, Cletus, try to get her back—or at least to get word of her—and to alleviate the pain. This trio of lovingly described characters journeys from intense grief to the understanding that love is never truly lost.

HONORS

What Hearts by **Bruce Brooks. LAURA GERINGER/HARPERCOLLINS.**

Seven-year-old Asa, by far the best in his class, comes home from the last day of school with a knapsack full of prizes to find that his whole world has changed. Asa tries to make sense of a world in which he is challenged and put down by a domineering stepfather and only partially sustained by his loving but disturbed mother. Four stories show Asa at seven, nine, eleven, and twelve, struggling to find the secret of connection with others.

The Dark-thirty: Southern Tales of the Supernatural by **Patricia C. McKissack. KNOPF.**

The dark-thirty is that special half hour of twilight, just before dark, when everyone hurries home because the spirits and monsters come out. This collection of spine-tingling tales ranges from the time of slavery to the civil rights movement. Strong characterization, classic themes, and suspenseful plots are strongly crafted in the oral tradition of African-American folklore.

Somewhere in the Darkness by **Walter Dean Myers. SCHOLASTIC.**

Jimmy Little had always wanted a father. However, when Crab, his father, who is virtually a stranger, appears in a dark hallway straight from a prison hospital, it is not at all what he had hoped for. On the tense, frightening trip with Crab to Chicago and then to Alabama, Jimmy finds he must learn self-knowledge as well as compassion to deal with a difficult and dangerous situation.

1992 AWARD

Shiloh by **Phyllis Reynolds Naylor. ATHENEUM.**

Marty Preston, an eleven-year-old West Virginian boy, befriends a stray dog and while protecting the dog from abuse wrestles with universal questions of honesty, commitment, and ethical decision making. Marty discovers that discerning right from wrong is not as straightforward as he had imagined.

HONORS

Nothing But the Truth: A Documentary Novel **by Avi. ORCHARD.**

Avi's documentary approach chronicles the results of a teacher's objection to a ninth grader's humming along with "The Star Spangled Banner." School rules stipulate that students are to stand at "respectful, silent attention." Miscommunication, misperceptions, and personal viewpoints of right, wrong, and protected freedoms propel the characters rapidly into a crisis situation that forces the reader to explore issues of perception, reality, bias, and expediency.

The Wright Brothers: How They Invented the Airplane **by Russell Freedman, illustrated with original photographs by Wilbur and Orville Wright. HOLIDAY HOUSE.**

In a spirited blend of science, history, and biography, Freedman presents a fascinating portrait of a new age. Using Wilber and Orville Wright's own photographs as well as excerpts from their notes and journals, he creates a uniquely personal and engaging view of their accomplishments.

1991 AWARD

Maniac Magee **by Jerry Spinelli. LITTLE, BROWN.**

Jeffrey Lionel Magee is a legendary character who runs the rails faster than other kids run the ground. Jeffrey bunts "the world's first frogball for a four-bagger" and performs other amazing feats.

HONOR

The True Confessions of Charlotte Doyle **by Avi. ORCHARD.**

Avi weaves a finely crafted tale of high seas adventure and gripping suspense, made rich by thirteen-year-old Charlotte's deepening understanding of honor and herself.

1990 AWARD

Number the Stars **by Lois Lowry. HOUGHTON MIFFLIN.**

When ten-year-old Annemarie Johansen's family decides to pretend that her friend Ellen Rosen is her sister, they become involved in the effort to save the Danish Jews from the Nazis. As the author deftly portrays deep friendship, a strong family, and heroism in wartime, the story builds to a tense climax.

HONORS

Afternoon of the Elves by Janet Taylor Lisle. ORCHARD.

Fascinated by Sarah-Kate's backyard elf village, Hillary is unprepared for the secret side of the older girl's life. Strong, tough, an outcast at school, Sarah-Kate has been doing whatever she must to care for herself and her mentally ill mother. When her plight is discovered by adults, disturbing but necessary changes occur.

The Winter Room by Gary Paulsen. ORCHARD.

From the first page to the last, this story of farm life in northern Minnesota is so engrossing that the place and the people seem real. Eldon, the eleven-year-old narrator, takes the reader through the seasons and into the winter room, where stories are "not for believing so much, as to be believed in."

Shabanu, Daughter of the Wind by Suzanne Fisher Staples. KNOPF.

Spirited and courageous Shabanu, younger daughter of present-day Pakistani camel herders, loves her family's life and her role in caring for their camels. Both Shabanu and her older sister are betrothed to brothers, but as her sister's wedding nears, a calamity occurs that changes forever the life of independent Shabanu.

1989 AWARD

Joyful Noise: Poems for Two Voices by Paul Fleischman, illustrated by Eric Beddows. CHARLOTTE ZOLOTOW/HARPER & ROW.

Fourteen poems, using two voices, sometimes alternating, sometimes together, offer listeners a look at what insects just might think of themselves and their world. The book lice, grasshoppers, house crickets, and their poetic companions are illustrated in soft yet often comical black-and-white pencil drawings.

HONORS

In the Beginning: Creation Stories from Around the World by Virginia Hamilton, illustrated by Barry Moser. HARCOURT BRACE JOVANOVICH.

Stories from African, Chinese, Native American, and Guinean peoples are represented among the twenty-five creation myths found in this collection. Faithfully retold, the stories are followed by notes about their sources. Dramatic watercolor paintings accent each tale.

Scorpions by Walter Dean Myers. HARPER & ROW.

Hoping to find a way to raise money for an appeal for his imprisoned older brother, twelve-year-old Jamal agrees to try to become the leader of his brother's Harlem gang, the Scorpions. Involvement with the gang (and the gun he is given) leads to tragedy for Jamal and his friend Tito.

1988 AWARD

Lincoln: A Photobiography **by Russell Freedman. CLARION.**

An ambitious man, Lincoln struggled hard to get an education, to build his law practice, and to become politically successful. The man, his wit, and his wisdom are vividly and honestly portrayed in this straightforward biography and its ninety photographs.

HONORS

After the Rain **by Norma Fox Mazer. MORROW.**

Fifteen-year-old Rachel tries to balance her concern for her own life with her grandfather's need for her help. Never close to the old man, she slowly comes to love him. As she struggles to help him maintain his independence, he weakens and nears death.

Hatchet **by Gary Paulsen. BRADBURY.**

When the pilot dies of a heart attack, Brian crash-lands the small plane in the Canadian wilderness. Left with only a hatchet and the clothes he is wearing, Brian begins a gripping fifty-four-day ordeal that challenges his physical and psychological skills to their limits.

1987 AWARD

The Whipping Boy **by Sid Fleischman, illustrated by Peter Sís. GREENWILLOW.**

Whenever Prince Brat does anything bad, Jemmy, his whipping boy, is punished. The spoiled prince decides to run away from the palace, forcing Jemmy to go with him. Far from the safety of the court, the prince quickly learns how little he knows about the outside world and how important Jemmy is to his survival.

HONORS

On My Honor **by Marion Dane Bauer. CLARION.**

Before leaving on a bike ride with his impetuous friend Tony, Joel gives his father his word of honor that he will not swim in a river known to be dangerous. Tony convinces Joel that the river is safe; the two swim; and Tony drowns. Joel is left alone to face his guilt, both sets of parents, and his own grief.

Volcano: The Eruption and Healing of Mount St. Helens **by Patricia Lauber. BRADBURY.**

The eruption of Mount St. Helens and the subsequent regrowth of plants are vividly portrayed in color photographs and a dynamic text. The volcanic eruption is seen not as just a disaster, but as a builder of life on this planet.

A Fine White Dust by **Cynthia Rylant**. BRADBURY.

Although neither his parents nor his best friend are particularly religious, Peter feels a need for something deeper than just churchgoing. When an itinerant preacher comes to town, Peter is mesmerized by the man and "saved." Invited to go away with the preacher, Peter reluctantly agrees, only to be left behind and forgotten.

1986 AWARD

Sarah, Plain and Tall by **Patricia MacLachlan**. HARPER & ROW.

Life on the prairie with two children and no wife is lonely and difficult, so Caleb and Anna's father advertises for a wife. Sarah answers his ad and soon agrees to come all the way from Maine for a visit. Captivated by her, Anna and Caleb worry that Sarah misses the sea too much to stay with them.

HONORS

Commodore Perry in the Land of the Shogun by **Rhoda Blumberg**. LOTHROP.

Commodore Perry's fascinating mission to Japan in 1853 is told at a lively pace, with special attention given to the negotiating skill that led to his success; to his sensitivity to cultural differences; and to his just plain curiosity. The accompanying pictures include many sketched by the Japanese and the Americans who were with Matthew Perry.

Dogsong by **Gary Paulsen**. BRADBURY.

Unhappy with the snowmobile-and-television society that seems to have taken over his Eskimo village, Russell turns to Oogruk, the old man of the village, for help in finding a path back to the old ways. With Oogruk's advice and encouragement, Russell begins an arduous dogsled journey northward to find his own "song."

1985 AWARD

The Hero and the Crown by **Robin McKinley**. GREENWILLOW.

The daughter of the king of Damar and his second wife (a witch woman from the north), Aerin does not fit in at court. Unable to succeed her father to the throne, she must instead find her own destiny. Wielding her blue sword, she not only defeats dragons but finally becomes the hero of the kingdom.

HONORS

The Moves Make the Man by **Bruce Brooks**. HARPER & ROW.

The first black to go to the formerly all-white junior high school, Jerome is a passionate basketball player. When he meets Bix Rivers, an unstable outsider who is a gifted athlete, Jerome decides to teach him basketball. As they play the game, Bix's mental illness becomes more apparent, and Jerome is less able to help him.

One-Eyed Cat by Paula Fox. BRADBURY.

After his minister father takes his new air rifle away from him and puts it in the attic, Ned sneaks upstairs, takes it, fires it once, and is terrified that he may have hit a cat. Struggling with his guilt, he tells one lie after another until he cannot bear it anymore and must confess to someone.

Like Jake and Me by Mavis Jukes, illustrated by Lloyd Bloom. KNOPF.

Alex wants to be liked by his rugged cowboy stepfather, but there are still barriers between the two. When Alex notices a wolf spider on Jake's neck and calmly mentions it, the rugged cowboy totally panics, admitting his terror of spiders. Alex comes to the rescue, and the two finally come to appreciate each other and their differences.

1984 AWARD

Dear Mr. Henshaw by Beverly Cleary, illustrated by Paul O. Zelinsky. MORROW.

Leigh Botts starts writing to the author of *Ways to Amuse a Dog* in second grade. Year after year the letters, and then a diary, become vehicles for expressing his feelings about himself, his parents' divorce, and his problems in school. Leigh's growth and acceptance of the divorce are tempered with much humor.

HONORS

The Wish Giver: Three Tales of Coven Tree by Bill Brittain, illustrated by
Andrew Glass. HARPER & ROW.

Thaddeus Blinn, the wish giver, sells Polly, Rowena, Henry, and Stew Meat wishes. All they have to do is hold the white card with the dot and wish carefully. The first three make their wishes with dire but comical consequences and leave Stew Meat to use his to undo everything they have done.

Sugaring Time by Kathryn Lasky, photographs by Christopher G. Knight.
MACMILLAN.

The author and photographer record a family's old-fashioned method of sugaring. When the right time finally comes, family members tap the maple trees, boil the sap, and enjoy a sugar-on-snow party and a pancake breakfast. The family's enjoyment of sugaring is evident in the often poetic text and the clear black-and-white photographs.

The Sign of the Beaver by Elizabeth George Speare. HOUGHTON MIFFLIN.

Left alone in the Maine wilderness, Matt first loses his rifle and food and then is savagely stung by bees. Found by Saknis, chief of the Beaver tribe, Matt is cared for in exchange for teaching the chief's grandson to read. As the boys' friendship develops, Matt gains an appreciation for the heritage and skills of the Beaver tribe.

A Solitary Blue by **Cynthia Voigt.** ATHENEUM.

Abandoned at the age of seven by his cause-conscious mother, Jeff is left to fend for himself and take care of his absent-minded-professor father. Not until Jeff is stricken with pneumonia at the age of twelve does his father understand how he, too, has deserted his son. Slowly the two build a close, strong relationship that is able to help them survive and grow.

1983 AWARD

Dicey's Song by **Cynthia Voigt.** ATHENEUM.

Finally settled in with Gram Tillerman while their mother is in a mental hospital, Dicey and her brothers and sisters discover that it is not easy to become a family. They must learn to love and trust Gram—and she them—while they try to adjust to a new school and make friends.

HONORS

Graven Images: Three Stories by **Paul Fleischman, illustrated by Andrew Glass.** HARPER & ROW.

Three gripping stories, two sinister and one funny and all with historical settings, are centered on graven images: a wooden boy with a frightening secret, a weathervane that leads to true love, and a statue ordered by a ghost.

Homesick: My Own Story by **Jean Fritz, illustrated by Margot Tomes and with photographs.** PUTNAM.

Fritz remembers with humor and poignancy two years of her childhood in China during the turbulent 1920s. She contends with being a "foreign devil," losing a longed-for baby sister, and, most of all, longing for the United States, a country she has never seen.

Sweet Whispers, Brother Rush by **Virginia Hamilton.** PHILOMEL.

Life changes radically for fourteen-year-old Tree and her older retarded brother when the ghost of Brother Rush appears to Tree, first in the street and then in her home. The handsome ghost of her mother's brother takes her back in time to bear witness to the past and to learn about the terrible disease that is killing her own brother.

The Blue Sword by **Robin McKinley.** GREENWILLOW.

Angharad Crewe is yanked out of an easy life on a Homelander outpost and thrust into one of rigorous training for her prophesied role as deliverer of the Hillfolk. She earns the right to carry the Blue Sword into battle, and with it she heroically leads a small band of warriors against the nonhuman Northerners.

Doctor De Soto by **William Steig, illustrated by the author.** FARRAR STRAUS GIROUX.

As mice dentists, the diminutive De Sotos have always refused to treat dangerous animals until a miserable fox appears begging for help. The compassionate mice cleverly find a way to rid the fox of his pain while guaranteeing their own safety.

1982 AWARD

A Visit to William Blake's Inn: Poems for Innocent and Experienced Travelers **by Nancy Willard, illustrated by Alice and Martin Provensen.** HARCOURT BRACE JOVANOVICH.

Written in the spirit of William Blake, these magical poems are built around the visit of a child to Blake's inn. It is staffed by mighty dragons that brew and bake, angels that wash feather beds, and animals that dance to the music of the Marmalade Man.

HONORS

Ramona Quimby, Age 8 by **Beverly Cleary, illustrated by Alan Tiegreen.** MORROW.

Ramona is now starting the third grade and her life is full of the usual hilarious trials that cause her to be labeled a "nuisance and show-off" by her new teacher. Whether she is deciding if she prefers her printed Q to the floppy cursive one, getting raw egg in her hair, or facing an interminably boring Sunday, Ramona is always a memorable character.

Upon the Head of the Goat: A Childhood in Hungary 1939–1944 by **Aranka Siegal.** FARRAR STRAUS GIROUX.

The destruction of nine-year-old Piri's family begins with Hungary's occupation by the Nazis. Her mother valiantly tries to keep the family together and safe, but one loss after another occurs until they board trains that will take them to Auschwitz. Siegal's book is a powerful autobiography.

1981 AWARD

Jacob Have I Loved by **Katherine Paterson.** CROWELL.

Although she takes pride in her twin sister's singing talent, Wheeze (Louise) is jealous of the attention Caroline gets on their Chesapeake Bay island. It is only when she leaves and starts a life as a midwife in Kentucky that Wheeze comes to understand that she has always been loved and accepted for herself.

HONORS

The Fledgling by Jane Langton, illustrated by Erik Blegvad. HARPER & ROW.

Frail young Georgie, almost light enough to blow away, is obsessed with her belief that she can fly. When a large Canada goose she has befriended hoots outside her window, Georgie hops on his back and flies away. Night after night they soar above Walden Pond until one misfortune and then another end Georgie's flying forever.

A Ring of Endless Light by Madeleine L'Engle. FARRAR STRAUS GIROUX.

Sixteen-year-old Vicky and her family spend the summer on a New England island with her dying grandfather. All summer long she and her family are preoccupied with the mysteries of life, death, and eternity, yet there is still time for Vicky to help with a Marine Biology Station dolphin project and to date two boys.

1980 AWARD

A Gathering of Days: A New England Girl's Journal, 1830–32 by Joan W. Blos. SCRIBNER.

Catherine Cabot Hall sporadically writes in her journal, filling it with recipes, excerpts from her copy book, secrets, fears, confidences, details of her adjustment to her stepmother, and thoughts on the pain of a friend's death. Though fiction, the journal is believable, and Catherine is easy to like.

HONOR

The Road from Home: The Story of an Armenian Girl by David Kherdian. GREENWILLOW.

After the Turks finish with their slaughter of nearly two million Armenians, Veron is the only survivor of her immediate family. When the Greeks attack Turkey, Veron and her aunt and cousin escape to Greece, and from there she travels to the United States, a mail-order bride and the future mother of the author.

1979 AWARD

The Westing Game by Ellen Raskin. DUTTON.

An expensive apartment building mysteriously fills up with sixteen occupants—all named as heirs or possible murderers in millionaire Sam Westing's will. The sixteen are paired, given $10,000, and challenged to discover who really killed Sam Westing.

Published in a new edition with an introduction by Ann Durrell in 2003 (Dutton).

HONOR

The Great Gilly Hopkins by Katherine Paterson. CROWELL.

Abandoned as a preschooler, Gilly has gone through a succession of foster homes. Smart, self-sufficient, and superficially hard, Gilly manages to do just what she wants until she is sent to stay with Maime Trotter, a woman with a big heart, patience, and wisdom enough to know how to reach the unhappy girl.

1978 AWARD

Bridge to Terabithia by Katherine Paterson, illustrated by Donna Diamond. CROWELL.

After practicing all summer to be the fastest runner in school, Jess is beaten by the new girl, Leslie. Gradually the two become close friends, creating an imaginary world in the woods and calling it Terabithia. When tragedy strikes, Jess, shocked and despairing, slowly begins to see the wonders Leslie left him.

HONORS

Ramona and Her Father by Beverly Cleary, illustrated by Alan Tiegreen. MORROW.

Ramona is in second grade when her father loses his job and her mother begins to work full-time. Ramona tries her best to help her family through the crisis, even starting a campaign to get her father to quit smoking. Her worries, problems, and joys, presented with lively good humor, are common to many children her age.

Anpao: An American Indian Odyssey by Jamake Highwater, illustrated by Fritz Scholder. LIPPINCOTT.

A beautiful Indian maiden promises to marry Anpao, but first he must get the Sun's permission and have him remove the ugly scar on his face. As Anpao travels the world looking for the Sun, he hears stories about his own roots as well as legends and myths of his people.

1977 AWARD

Roll of Thunder, Hear My Cry by Mildred D. Taylor, frontispiece by Jerry Pinkney. DIAL.

Cassie Logan and her brothers are part of a warm, intelligent, and courageous black family in rural Mississippi during the Depression. They try to maintain their pride as they take abuse from white children and then recognize that their personal difficulties are only symptoms of greater problems within their community.

Published in a new edition with a foreword by the author in 2001 (Phyllis J. Fogelman).

HONORS

A String in the Harp by Nancy Bond. MARGARET K. MCELDERRY/ATHENEUM.

Their father's remoteness and the strangeness of school in Wales make the children's adjustment to their mother's death even more difficult. Then twelve-year-old Peter finds an ancient harp key that pulls him back into Welsh history, helping him discover a purpose to living.

Abel's Island by William Steig, illustrated by the author. FARRAR STRAUS GIROUX.

After a violent storm, Abel, a mouse, finds himself alone, bewildered, and far, far away from his beloved wife Amanda. Sustained by his love for his wife, Abel uses all his resources to survive for a year on the deserted island.

1976 AWARD

The Grey King by Susan Cooper, illustrated by Michael Heslop. MARGARET K. MCELDERRY/ATHENEUM.

In Wales recovering from a serious illness, eleven-year-old Will, the youngest of the Old Ones, uses his considerable powers to find the golden harp that will awaken the Sleepers. It is not an easy quest, and Will has only the mysterious Bran and Bran's dog, Cafall, to help him fight the forces of dark and evil.

HONORS

The Hundred Penny Box by Sharon Bell Mathis, illustrated by Leo and Diane Dillon. VIKING.

For each of her hundred years there is a penny in Aunt Dew's box and a story to go along with it. More than his parents, Michael understands the importance of the box to the old woman and loves to hear her tell the stories again and again.

Dragonwings by Laurence Yep. HARPER & ROW.

In 1903 Moonshadow leaves the Middle Kingdom to join his father in San Francisco. To make the father's dream of building an aeroplane come true, the two of them leave the close-knit community that shelters their Chinese culture to live among white demons. Humorous accommodations are made between the different cultures as they grow in understanding and friendship.

1975 AWARD

M. C. Higgins, the Great by Virginia Hamilton. MACMILLAN.

Up on Sarah's Mountain, M. C. dreams of a way for his family to escape the spoil heap that may one day destroy their home. It is not his dreams but the boy's own strength and determination that help the family find a way to keep themselves safe.

Published in a new edition with an introduction by the author in 1999 (Simon & Schuster).

HONORS

My Brother Sam Is Dead by James Lincoln Collier and Christopher Collier. FOUR WINDS.

Tim's older brother, Sam, defies their father and runs off to join the Continental Army. When their father is imprisoned by the rebels and dies and Sam is hung by his own army, Tim sees how devastating war can be.

Philip Hall Likes Me, I Reckon Maybe by Bette Greene, illustrated by Charles Lilly. DIAL.

Eleven-year-old Beth Lambert, a spunky heroine, realizes she has been letting Philip Hall be number one in school because she is afraid he will not like her if she surpasses him. With gentle prodding from her family, Beth decides to go ahead and do her best—even if it means beating Philip Hall.

The Perilous Gard by Elizabeth Marie Pope, illustrated by Richard Cuffari. HOUGHTON MIFFLIN.

Banished by Queen Mary to the remote castle of Elvenwood, Kate Sutton quickly learns the castle's secret: It guards the last practitioners of the old religions. To keep their power, the fairy folk decide to sacrifice the man Kate loves on All Hallow's Eve.

Figgs & Phantoms by Ellen Raskin. DUTTON.

Mona is embarrassed by her zany, ex-show-business family—except for her four-foot-four-inch-tall Uncle Florence Italy Figg. When he dies, Mona is desolate. She is sure he has gone to Capri, the Figg family Heaven, and decides to follow him.

1974 AWARD

The Slave Dancer by Paula Fox, illustrated by Eros Keith. BRADBURY.

Kidnapped and forced to play his fife while the slaves "dance," thirteen-year-old Jessie learns all too soon about the savagery of the slave trade. For four long months he lives with the crew's cruelty until a storm wrecks the ship and Jessie and Ras, a would-be slave, are the only survivors.

Published in a new edition in 2001 (Richard Jackson/Atheneum).

HONOR

The Dark Is Rising **by Susan Cooper, illustrated by Alan E. Cober. MARGARET K. McELDERRY/ATHENEUM.**

On midwinter's eve, Will's eleventh birthday, the world is in turmoil with strange creatures appearing and stranger things happening. Will, the last of the Old Ones to be born, must use all his knowledge and skill to help in the fight against the Dark.

1973 AWARD

Julie of the Wolves **by Jean Craighead George, illustrated by John Schoenherr. HARPER & ROW.**

Having run away from a forced marriage, thirteen-year-old Miyax, an Eskimo, becomes lost on the Arctic plain. Her only hope for survival is acceptance by a wolf pack. Imitating their facial expressions and body movements, Miyax slowly becomes one of them, while still trying to get to safety.

HONORS

Frog and Toad Together **by Arnold Lobel, illustrated by the author. HARPER & ROW.**

Whether they are testing their willpower with a bowl of cookies or their patience while waiting for seeds to grow, Frog and Toad delight in each other's company. Witty, easy-to-read, and full of warmth and gentle humor, these five stories engagingly explore the meaning of friendship.

The Upstairs Room **by Johanna Reiss. CROWELL.**

As the German occupation of Holland tightens, two Jewish sisters are forced to hide in a secret upstairs room in an old farmhouse for two years. The girls experience fear, hope, terror, and boredom in their daily life and depend on the kindness and courage of others for their survival.

The Witches of Worm **by Zilpha Keatley Snyder, illustrated by Alton Raible. ATHENEUM.**

Deserted by her friends and her mother, Jessica channels her anger at life into "evil acts" that her cat, Worm, supposedly forces her to perform. Convinced first that Worm is a witch's cat, then that she is a witch, Jessica is ultimately forced to face herself and her feelings.

1972 AWARD

Mrs. Frisby and the Rats of NIMH by Robert C. O'Brien, pseud. (Robert Leslie Conly), illustrated by Zena Bernstein. ATHENEUM.

When nothing she does seems to help her son Timothy get well, Mrs. Frisby, a widowed mouse, turns to a colony of super-intelligent rats for help. The rats' high intelligence is the result of experiments performed upon them by human scientists at NIMH. Now the rats are intent upon starting a new civilization free from human interference.

HONORS

Incident at Hawk's Hill by Allan W. Eckert, illustrated by John Schoenherr. LITTLE, BROWN.

Lonely, small, and frail, six-year-old Ben shies away from people but shows deep interest in and affinity toward animals. Lost during a storm, he takes refuge with a badger who has just lost her young. The badger adopts him, and he lives a feral life for three months until he is found. Convincingly written, the incident is based on an actual occurrence in 1870.

The Planet of Junior Brown by Virginia Hamilton. MACMILLAN.

For more than two months, huge, musical genius Junior Brown and his friend and protector Buddy Clark have been cutting classes and hiding in a secret basement room created by the school custodian. Buddy and Mr. Poole, the custodian, are trying desperately to help Junior, who seems to be slipping slowly but inexorably into madness.

The Tombs of Atuan by Ursula K. LeGuin, illustrated by Gail Garraty. ATHENEUM.

From the time Tenar was five, her life has been focused on the tombs and her future as their priestess. Renamed Arha, she guards the labyrinthine tunnels, knowing that they hide great treasure. When she finds a man (Ged of *A Wizard of Earthsea*) in the tunnels seeking the other half to the Ring of Erreth-Akbe, Arha is torn between her duty to kill him and her compassion for him.

Annie and the Old One by Miska Miles, illustrated by Peter Parnall. LITTLE, BROWN.

Annie likes her life the way it is with her mother weaving, her father making jewelry, and her grandmother, the Old One, always there to tell her stories and to help with chores. When grandmother announces that she will die when the new rug is finished, Annie tries desperately to stop the inevitable by secretly unraveling the rug.

The Headless Cupid by Zilpha Keatley Snyder, illustrated by Alton Raible. ATHENEUM.

Eleven-year-old David is pleased about his father's remarriage until he meets his new stepsister, Amanda, a self-proclaimed witch. Angry at her mother for remarrying, Amanda sets up situations that lead the other children to believe their house is haunted. Then unexplained events turn the tables, frightening even Amanda.

1971 AWARD

The Summer of the Swans by Betsy Byars, illustrated by Ted CoConis. VIKING.

An insecure fourteen-year-old, Sarah is unhappy with herself and her family. Though she loves her mentally disabled brother Charlie, Sarah is tired of always being responsible for him. When Charlie turns up missing, however, Sarah tries desperately to find him and in the process discovers that she is less the ugly duckling than she had supposed.

HONORS

Knee Knock Rise by Natalie Babbitt. FARRAR STRAUS GIROUX.

In this tale filled with folk humor, Egan goes to the village for a visit and becomes intrigued with the tales and wails of a monster that lives in the peaks of Knee Knock Rise. After an unprecedented climb up the mountain, Egan discovers the practical explanation for the legendary creature. The villagers refuse to listen to him, preferring to let their folklore live on as history.

Enchantress from the Stars by Sylvia Louise Engdahl, illustrated by Rodney Shackell. ATHENEUM.

Invaded by technologically advanced Imperials, the Andrecians are close to being destroyed by their occupiers when beings from an even more highly advanced civilization decide to intervene secretly. Using their telekenetic powers, three Federation members pose as magicians, teaching a young Andrecian how to use his psychic abilities to combat the invaders.

Sing Down the Moon by Scott O'Dell. HOUGHTON MIFFLIN.

At fourteen, Bright Morning dares to be optimistic about her future. Her mother is a wealthy Navajo, and Bright Morning is to marry Tall Boy, a young Navajo warrior. Then she is wrenched from her home by Spanish slavers. When freed, she is uprooted again, this time by the cavalry, who force the Navajo to make a 300-mile march to Bosque Redondo.

1970 AWARD

Sounder by William H. Armstrong, illustrated by James Barkley. HARPER & ROW.

Sounder, the family dog, valiantly defends the father when the sheriff and his deputies come to arrest him for stealing food for his starving family. Years later, the dog, shot and maimed by the deputies, is the only one to recognize the father when he returns, paralyzed and deformed.

HONORS

Our Eddie by Sulamith Ish-Kishor. PANTHEON.

Eddie's father is a stern, insensitive zealot who refuses, until it is too late, to see that his son is gradually succumbing to a debilitating disease. Set in London and New York in the 1920s, most of this story of a warm Jewish immigrant family is told by Eddie's insightful sister.

The Many Ways of Seeing: An Introduction to the Pleasures of Art by Janet Gaylord Moore, illustrated with black-and-white and color reproductions and photographs. WORLD.

Moore, of the Cleveland Museum of Art, encourages readers to try a new way of approaching art: to see art reflecting the world and nature, and the world in turn reflecting art. Paintings (reproduced in color), poems, and quotations are arranged to lead to the discovery of new comparisons between modern, traditional, or ancient art and the imagery of word and picture.

Journey Outside by Mary Q. Steele, illustrated by Rocco Negri. VIKING.

In a story filled with allegory and symbolism, Dilar's people endlessly travel an underground river, headed for the "better place." But Dilar, suspecting that they are merely going around in circles, jumps from his raft and accidentally makes his way into the outside world. There, nearly blinded by the light, he tries to learn more about his people and to find a way to bring them aboveground.

1969 AWARD

The High King by Lloyd Alexander. HOLT RINEHART & WINSTON.

In the final book of the chronicles of Prydain, Taran leads his forces against Arawn and his army of the dead. Victorious, but with great loss of life and destruction to Prydain, Taran becomes High King, fulfilling the predictions of his wizard guardian, Dallben.

Published in a new edition with a pronunciation guide in 1999 (Henry Holt).

HONORS

To Be a Slave by Julius Lester, illustrated by Tom Feelings. DIAL.

American slaves, runaways, and emancipated people provide a powerful testament of how they felt about slavery and what they endured. The author dynamically blends quotations from published and unpublished sources and presents them in rough chronological order.

When Shlemiel Went to Warsaw and Other Stories by Isaac Bashevis Singer, illustrated by Margot Zemach. FARRAR STRAUS GIROUX.

In eight delightfully silly stories, five retold from the Yiddish and three original, readers are introduced to a memorable collection of characters. Among them are a mixed-up Shlemiel, who does not recognize his wife and village, and Utzel's daughter, Poverty, who seems to grow larger as he grows poorer.

1968 AWARD

From the Mixed-Up Files of Mrs. Basil E. Frankweiler by E. L. Konigsburg, illustrated by the author. ATHENEUM.

Having carefully planned how and to where they will run away, Claudia and her little brother, James (and his money), board a bus, head to New York City, and go to the Metropolitan Museum of Art. There they hide in washrooms, sleep on ancient beds, and get involved in solving an exciting mystery.

HONORS

Jennifer, Hecate, Macbeth, William McKinley, and Me, Elizabeth by E. L. Konigsburg, illustrated by the author. ATHENEUM.

Elizabeth is lonely at her new school until she meets Jennifer, a girl her age who claims to be a real witch. In awe of Jennifer, Elizabeth agrees to become her apprentice and initially finds her boring life full of adventure. But Jennifer is very demanding, and even superficially docile Elizabeth can only be pushed so far.

The Black Pearl by Scott O'Dell, illustrated by Milton Johnson. HOUGHTON MIFFLIN.

In this story written with stark simplicity and riveting suspense, Ramon confronts his two greatest enemies in the waters of Baja California. The legendary curse of the Manta Diablo holds true when Ramon wrests the fabulous black pearl from the Manta's cave and his life is changed forever.

The Fearsome Inn by Isaac Bashevis Singer, illustrated by Nonny Hogrogian. SCRIBNER.

Unaware that the owners of the inn are a witch and her half-devil husband, three young men seek shelter there on a stormy winter night. One of the three, a clever student of the Cabala, recognizes the couple's evil and courageously defeats them, sending the pair "behind the Mountains of Darkness where there is neither day nor night."

The Egypt Game by Zilpha Keatley Snyder, illustrated by Alton Raible. ATHENEUM.

April and Melanie begin the Egypt game in the backyard of a slightly sinister curio shop. With costumes, ceremonies, an evil god, an oracular owl, and four other members, the game is seriously and imaginatively played. After the murder of a child, they are forced inside for awhile, but finally they begin the game again. This time one of the players almost becomes the next victim.

1967 AWARD

Up a Road Slowly by Irene Hunt, cover painting by Don Bolognese. FOLLETT.

When Julie is seven, her mother dies. She and her little brother are sent to live with her strict, schoolteacher aunt. Through the years, Julie keeps hoping that her father will want them back, that staying with Aunt Cordelia is just temporary, but slowly she comes to love her aunt and wants to stay.

HONORS

The King's Fifth by Scott O'Dell, illustrated by Samuel Bryant. HOUGHTON MIFFLIN.

Imprisoned in Vera Cruz and awaiting trial, seventeen-year-old Esteban tells of his part in the disastrous expedition for gold to the Seven Cities of Cibola. A mapmaker, Esteban is left with the bags of gold. After seeing the greed, cruelty, and, finally, death of those searching for it, he throws the gold into a volcanic crater.

Zlateh the Goat and Other Stories by Isaac Bashevis Singer, illustrated by Maurice Sendak, translated from the Yiddish by the author and Elizabeth Shub. HARPER & ROW.

Seven stories rich with eastern European culture and Jewish folklore are filled with lively characters, delightfully funny fools, clever people, and loyal animals. The ink drawings of Sendak create wonderful scenes complementing the stories perfectly.

The Jazz Man by Mary Hays Weik, illustrated by Ann Grifalconi. ATHENEUM.

Night after night Zeke and his mother and father listen to the jazz man play his piano. Then his mother tires of his father not working, and she leaves them. Soon his father goes as well, and Zeke is alone. As the gloomy days and nights pass, Zeke dreams of the jazz man and of better, happier times.

1966 AWARD

I, Juan de Pareja by **Elizabeth Borton de Treviño**. FARRAR STRAUS GIROUX.

Behind the great painter Velasquez stands his faithful slave, Juan, ready to prepare a canvas, mix paint, and boost his morale. But, secretly, Juan teaches himself to paint, winning his freedom and the respect of a great master.

HONORS

The Black Cauldron by **Lloyd Alexander**. HOLT RINEHART & WINSTON.

Assistant Pig-Keeper Taran excitedly joins Gwydion and the other men of Prydain in their attack on Arawn, Lord of Annuvin, and his cauldron-born army. Only by destroying the cauldron can they hope to stop Arawn and his deathless warriors from overrunning Prydain.

The Animal Family by **Randall Jarrell, illustrated by Maurice Sendak**. PANTHEON.

Isolated in his house by the sea, the hunter is lonely until the day he sees the mermaid. Together they form an amazing family with first a bear cub, then a lynx, and finally an orphaned boy. Each fits gently and beautifully into the very special world created by the unusual couple.

The Noonday Friends by **Mary Stolz, illustrated by Louis Glanzman**. HARPER & ROW.

Her hard-working mother and out-of-work father depend on Franny to take care of her little brother after school and to help out in other ways. The only time left for friendship is during lunch hour at school when she talks to Simone, a friend with whom she can share problems.

1965 AWARD

Shadow of a Bull by **Maia Wojciechowska, illustrated by Alvin Smith**. ATHENEUM.

With everyone waiting for him to become a great bullfighter like his father, Manolo is afraid to let them know that he has a different dream—to become a doctor. He trains and practices for the ring until finally he has the courage and confidence to admit that he can never be a bullfighter.

HONOR

Across Five Aprils by **Irene Hunt**. FOLLETT.

At nine, Jethro is excited by the prospect of a civil war coming to the country. When the nation really does go to war, his brothers and friends go in different directions, fighting for either the North or the South. Jethro begins to understand how devastating war really is to family and nation.

1964 AWARD

It's Like This, Cat by Emily Neville, illustrated by Emil Weiss. HARPER & ROW.

When his father suggests that owning a dog might be good for him, fourteen-year-old Dave defiantly goes to Aunt Kate the Cat Woman and adopts a stray. The cat ends up leading him to new people and adventures all over Manhattan—and even to an appreciation for his parents.

HONORS

Rascal: A Memoir of a Better Era by Sterling North, illustrated by John Schoenherr. DUTTON.

For twelve months Sterling owned the raccoon, raising him from a tiny captured kit to a large adult yearning for his freedom. Bright, curious, energetic, and endearing, Rascal fills the boy's life with love, companionship, and adventure during their year together.

The Loner by Ester Wier, illustrated by Christine Price. McKAY.

Both nameless and homeless, the boy wanders the country with other migrants, hoping to find work and food. Finally, lost and weak from hunger, he collapses and is found by a woman called The Boss. The gruff but gentle sheep rancher names him David and gives him a chance to make his own life on her Montana ranch.

1963 AWARD

A Wrinkle in Time by Madeleine L'Engle. Ariel / FARRAR STRAUS GIROUX.

Meg, Charles Wallace, and next-door neighbor Calvin go into space and through time to rescue Meg's father, a scientist who disappeared while working on a secret project. The children' intergalactic search leads them to a confrontation with the forces of evil on the planet Camazotz, where conformity means survival.

HONORS

Thistle and Thyme: Tales and Legends from Scotland by Sorche Nic Leodhas, pseud. (Leclaire Alger), illustrated by Evaline Ness. HOLT RINEHART & WINSTON.

Using her memories of stories told in her family, the author retells ten stories based on Scottish legends and folktales. Some are humorous, others mysterious and suspenseful, and all of them possess the rhythm of the Gaelic language.

Men of Athens by Olivia Coolidge, illustrated by Milton Johnson. HOUGHTON MIFFLIN.

The golden age of Greece comes to life through the men and women who lived during and immediately before and after that brief fifty-year period. The battles they waged to make Greece strong and free; the brilliance of the leading artists, philosophers, and statesmen; and the excitement of the time make exciting reading.

1962 AWARD

The Bronze Bow by Elizabeth George Speare. HOUGHTON MIFFLIN.

At the death of his parents, Daniel swears vengeance against the Roman invaders. For five years he hides in the mountains of Galilee with a band of rebels but finally must return to care for his sister. He meets Jesus but refuses to accept his message of love, wanting revenge instead. Only when all seems nearly lost does he start to understand the power of love.

HONORS

Frontier Living by Edwin Tunis, illustrated by the author. WORLD.

Beginning with the settlement of the Piedmont area in the early 1700s, nineteen distinct frontier movements take American settlers from the East Coast across the continent and through the nineteenth century. Details of daily life and carefully drawn pictures of the people and objects show what makes this era unique.

The Golden Goblet by Eloise Jarvis McGraw. COWARD.

Under the control of his cruel and unscrupulous half-brother, Gebu, Ranofer, a boy of ancient Egypt who lives in Thebes, is sent to work for a goldsmith. Slowly he discovers that Gebu is stealing gold objects from the Valley of the Tombs, and he must find a way to expose him.

Belling the Tiger by Mary Stolz, illustrated by Beni Montresor. HARPER.

Asa and Rambo, the two smallest mice, are given the dubious honor of belling the cat. While getting the bell, the two accidentally get stuck on a ship and travel to a tropical island where they "bell" a tiger. Home again, the diminutive duo have the courage to demand a raise in status.

1961 AWARD

Island of the Blue Dolphins by Scott O'Dell. HOUGHTON MIFFLIN.

Accidentally left behind when her tribe flees, Karana spends eighteen years alone on an island off the coast of California. Her courage and resourcefulness help her to survive and to fill her life with moments of beauty and happiness.

Published in a new edition with illustrations by Ted Lewin in 1990 (Houghton Mifflin).

HONORS

America Moves Forward: A History for Peter by Gerald W. Johnson, illustrated by Leonard Everett Fisher. MORROW.

From World War I to 1956, major events and important men of politics are evaluated and discussed for their impact on American life and history. The third and final volume in a work that offers a personalized look at American history, the book is illustrated with striking scratchboard pictures.

Old Ramon by Jack Schaefer, illustrated by Harold West. HOUGHTON MIFFLIN.

Old Ramon teaches the boy as much as he can during the months they spend with the sheep in the mountains. Along the way, Ramon shares stories of his youth as a shepherd with the boy's grandfather and brings the boy back to the valley with a keener understanding and appreciation for the life of a shepherd.

The Cricket in Times Square by George Selden, pseud. (George Thompson), illustrated by Garth Williams. FARRAR STRAUS GIROUX.

Accidentally brought into a New York City subway station, Chester Cricket is found by Mario Bellini, the son of a newsstand owner. Chester is befriended by two subway animals, Harry Cat and Tucker Mouse, who encourage him to use his musical talents to help the Bellinis. An overnight success, Chester nonetheless longs to return to the country.

1960 AWARD

Onion John by Joseph Krumgold, illustrated by Symeon Shimin. CROWELL.

Twelve-year-old Andy is torn between his love for his father and his affection for Onion John, the old man whose way of life is totally foreign to nearly everyone in town. When members of the Rotary Club try to build Onion John a new house, their actions have great repercussions.

HONORS

My Side of the Mountain by Jean Craighead George. DUTTON.

Tired of living in a crowded city apartment, Sam Gribley runs away from home and heads for his Grandpa Gribley's long-lost homestead in the Catskill Mountains. For a year he stays alone, learning to live off the land, hollowing out a tree for a home, taming a falcon, and using every bit of ingenuity and resourcefulness he has to survive.

America Is Born: A History for Peter by Gerald W. Johnson, illustrated by Leonard Everett Fisher. MORROW.

Johnson's account of America's history is a very personal retelling of the lives and adventures of the people who explored and settled this country. The first in a three-volume series, the book covers the time from Columbus to the Revolutionary War and the Constitutional Convention.

The Gammage Cup by Carol Kendall, illustrated by Erik Blegvad. HARCOURT BRACE.

Five misfits are sent into exile in the mountains when they refuse to conform to Minnepin traditions of dress, ideas, and lifestyle. They come to the rescue of the Land between the Mountains when they uncover an invasion plot by the Mushroom People.

1959 AWARD

The Witch of Blackbird Pond by Elizabeth George Speare. HOUGHTON MIFFLIN.

When her grandfather dies, sixteen-year-old Kit leaves the West Indies to live with her Puritan Aunt Rachel and her family. Kit's lively personality, her bright clothes, and her friendship with an outcast Quaker woman make her a target for charges of witchcraft in 1687 New England.

Published in a new edition with illustrations by Barry Moser in 2001 (Houghton Mifflin).

HONORS

The Family under the Bridge by Natalie Savage Carlson, illustrated by Garth Williams. HARPER.

Armand, who wanders the streets of Paris without a care, finds that his place beneath a bridge has been invaded by three children and their mother. Though he does not want to have anything to do with the children, the old man soon becomes a grandfather figure to the family, helping them, sharing the fun of the city, and ultimately making them his responsibility.

Along Came a Dog by Meindert DeJong, illustrated by Maurice Sendak. HARPER.

When her frostbitten toes fall off, the little red hen becomes a target for the other chickens' abuse. Only the big, homeless dog comes to her rescue, looking on her as something to guard and love as he tries to make the farm his home.

Chucaro: Wild Pony of the Pampa by Francis Kalnay, illustrated by Julian de Miskey. HARCOURT BRACE.

Once wild on the Argentine pampa, Chucaro is captured and tamed by Pedrito and his gaucho friend Juan. When the patron demands a gentle horse for his spoiled and cruel son, it is Chucaro he gets in spite of Pedrito's determination to keep him.

The Perilous Road by **William O. Steele, illustrated by Paul Galdone.**
HARCOURT BRACE.

Eleven-year-old Chris passionately hates the Yankees invading his Tennessee homeland and wants to do anything to help the South. He is deaf to his father's words
when he says war is the worst thing that can happen to people. Then Chris is caught
in the middle of a savage battle and realizes how horrible war really is.

1958 AWARD

Rifles for Watie by **Harold Keith.** CROWELL.

Sixteen-year-old Jeff, already a combat veteran in the Union Army and winner of
the Congressional Medal of Honor, is captured by the rebel troops of General Stand
Watie, a Cherokee Indian, and forced to become one of his scouts.

HONORS

Gone-Away Lake by **Elizabeth Enright, illustrated by Beth and Joe Krush.**
HARCOURT BRACE.

All summer Julian and his ten-year-old cousin Portia explore the houses they discover
around Gone-Away Lake. They tell no one about the place or the two old people living in one of the houses until a near tragedy exposes their secret.

Tom Paine, Freedom's Apostle by **Leo Gurko, illustrated by Fritz Kredel.** CROWELL.

With hardly any education or money and only Ben Franklin's letter of introduction,
Tom Paine goes to America and writes *Common Sense,* the first of his revolutionary
pamphlets. The power and vision of Paine's writings and the violent feelings they
aroused throughout his life are evident in this biography.

The Great Wheel by **Robert Lawson.** VIKING.

Aunt Honoria predicts that Conn will leave Ireland and head west. Now he is in
Chicago working on a construction project for a man named Ferris. His aunt has also
made the wild prediction that he will ride the world's biggest wheel. Conn does as
soon as Mr. Ferris's daring project is completed for the Chicago World's Columbian
Exposition of 1893.

The Horsecatcher by **Mari Sandoz.** WESTMINSTER.

Unlike the other Cheyenne boys, Young Elk refuses to kill. He wants to capture and
tame the wild horses of the prairie. When his father insists he join in their war, he
runs away, returning months later with fifteen horses and the start of what becomes
a nearly legendary way with wild horses.

1957 AWARD

Miracles on Maple Hill **by Virginia Sorensen, illustrated by Beth and Joe Krush.** HARCOURT BRACE.

When her father finally returns from being a prisoner of war, Marley's family decides to try to make a new beginning on a beautiful farm in Pennsylvania. During their first year there, they marvel at the miracle of the sap rising in the maple trees and the changes in each other.

Published in a new edition in 2003 (Harcourt).

HONORS

Black Fox of Lorne **by Marguerite de Angeli.** DOUBLEDAY.

Shipwrecked off the coast of medieval Scotland, identical twins Jan and Brus are the only ones left alive when their father and his men are murdered. They survive by tricking the Scots into thinking that only one of them exists. Having sworn to avenge their father's murder, they foil the man's treasonous plot and keep their vow.

The House of Sixty Fathers **by Meindert DeJong, illustrated by Maurice Sendak.** HARPER.

Alone in his family sampan, Tien Pao lands in Japanese-occupied China and begins a dangerous journey back to Hengyang during World War II. On his way, a company of American airmen adopt him, and he finds himself with sixty strange but kind fathers who help him find his family.

Old Yeller **by Fred Gipson, illustrated by Carl Burger.** HARPER.

Left to help care for the homestead while his father takes their cattle to Kansas, fourteen-year-old Travis initially resents the intrusion of the big yellow dog. The dog proves his worth by rescuing little Arliss from a bear and Travis from wild hogs, guaranteeing himself a home.

Mr. Justice Holmes **by Clara Ingram Judson, illustrated by Robert Todd.** FOLLETT.

The son of a famous writer, Oliver Wendell Holmes Jr. is a daydreamer whose brilliance is not always apparent to his family. After serving in the Civil War, he becomes a lawyer and a teacher, trying to make law interesting and clear to those entering the profession. Well-respected but never wealthy, he becomes one of the country's most highly esteemed Supreme Court justices.

The Corn Grows Ripe **by Dorothy Rhoads, illustrated by Jean Charlot.** VIKING.

A happy but often irresponsible twelve-year-old Yucatan boy must suddenly grow up when his father is injured. Tigre bravely goes to another village to get a bonesetter and then sets about clearing and burning the family's new cornfield, a ritualized duty that goes back to Mayan times. He proves he can be reliable.

1956 AWARD

Carry On, Mr. Bowditch by Jean Lee Latham, illustrated by
John O'Hara Cosgrave II. HOUGHTON MIFFLIN.

In spite of having little education, Nat Bowditch manages to teach himself mathematics and the principles of navigation. When he gets the chance to sail as a second mate, he teaches the rest of the crew to navigate and even finds mistakes in the navigational tables. He later rewrites the tables, and they become a standard navigational tool.

Published in a new edition in 2003 (Houghton Mifflin).

HONORS

The Golden Name Day by Jennie Lindquist, illustrated by Garth Williams.
HARPER.

Staying with her Swedish-American grandparents while her mother is hospitalized, Nancy is warmly welcomed into an extended family of aunts, uncles, and cousins. With everyone else having a special Swedish Name Day to celebrate, the family unsuccessfully tries to find a matching Swedish name for Nancy. Only when a new family moves in is Nancy's problem solved.

The Secret River by Marjorie Kinnan Rawlings, illustrated by Leonard Weisgard.
SCRIBNER.

When hard times come to the Florida forest people, little Calpurnia and her dog, Buggyhorse, go to the wise woman of the forest for help. Advised to follow her nose, Calpurnia discovers a beautiful river full of fish. She catches many and brings them home, making hard times "soft."

Men, Microscopes, and Living Things by Katherine Shippen, illustrated by
Anthony Ravielli. VIKING.

The author begins with Aristotle and his investigation of natural science, then moves on to Pliny, Harvey, Linnaeus, Lamarck, and others. The lively yet factual writing provides interesting insights into the work of significant biologists.

1955 AWARD

The Wheel on the School by Meindert DeJong, illustrated by Maurice Sendak.
HARPER.

Inspired by Lina's composition about storks, her classmates and teacher decide to find a way to bring the birds and their luck back to their little Dutch village. As the children involve the people of the village in the search for a wheel and for a way to attach it to their school, they bring their small community together.

HONORS

The Courage of Sarah Noble by Alice Dalgliesh, illustrated by Leonard Weisgard. SCRIBNER.

"Keep up your courage," Sarah's mother tells her when she leaves with her father to build a home in the wilderness. The home finished, Sarah stays with friendly Indians while her father goes back for the rest of the family.

Banner in the Sky: The Story of a Boy and a Mountain by James Ullman. LIPPINCOTT.

Although his father died trying to climb the Citadel, the highest mountain in the Alps, Rudy is determined to scale it himself. He hides his climbing ability from his mother and his Alpine-guide uncle and joins an English expedition hoping to be able to plant his father's red shirt at the top as a banner in the sky.

1954 AWARD

. . . And Now Miguel by Joseph Krumgold, illustrated by Jean Charlot. CROWELL.

Every spring Miguel hopes this is the year he will be asked to join the men as they take their sheep up into the Sangre de Cristo Mountains of New Mexico. When at the age of twelve he is told it is not yet time for him, he works hard and prays that his father will see how grown up he is.

HONORS

All Alone by Claire Huchet Bishop, illustrated by Feodor Rojankovsky. VIKING.

When his father sends him to the high pastures with the heifers, Marcel is forcefully reminded of the village motto, "Each man for himself." But loneliness makes the yodel of another boy welcome, and when disaster strikes, Marcel is saved by his willingness to help someone else.

Magic Maize by Mary and Conrad Buff, illustrated by the authors. HOUGHTON MIFFLIN.

With the gringo world encroaching on the old ways of the Indians of Guatemala, a father continues to teach his son the old ways of farming and of praying to the gods of planting and harvest. Yet when their crop fails, it is the gringos who come to the family's aid.

Hurry Home, Candy by Meindert DeJong, illustratedd by Maurice Sendak. HARPER.

Taken from his mother before he is weaned and given to a family that only knows how to hurt and control him, Candy is lost on a family outing and becomes a stray. He longs for his own home and for people who will really love him.

Shadrach **by Meindert DeJong, illustrated by Maurice Sendak. HARPER.**

After Davie's grandfather promises him a rabbit of his own, the little boy's excitement is nearly uncontainable. Davie bravely gathers food near a dangerous Dutch canal, helps get his hutch ready, and, when the rabbit arrives, lavishes attention and affection on the little animal.

Theodore Roosevelt, Fighting Patriot **by Clara Ingram Judson, illustrated by Lorence F. Bjorklund. FOLLETT.**

Independent and honorable, Theodore is forever facing challenges because of his poor health, bad vision, and determination to learn as much as he can. As an adult he is remembered for leading the Rough Riders up San Juan Hill, starting our national park system, and being a president with tremendous courage and integrity.

1953 AWARD

Secret of the Andes **by Ann Nolan Clark, illustrated by Jean Charlot. VIKING.**

Determined to discover another way of life, Cusi leaves his beautiful Incan home in the Andes Mountains and goes to the lowlands of Spanish Peru. Once there he longs for the hidden valley and the Old One. He returns knowing that he will never again willingly leave his home or break his vow to keep the Incan secret.

HONORS

The Bears on Hemlock Mountain **by Alice Dalgliesh, illustrated by Helen Sewell. SCRIBNER.**

"There are no bears on Hemlock Mountain, no bears at all," Jonathan repeats as he goes over the mountain to borrow the big iron pot. But on the way back, Jonathan learns that there are indeed bears on Hemlock Mountain.

Birthdays of Freedom, Vol. I **by Genevieve Foster, illustrated by the author. SCRIBNER.**

Starting with the excitement of the signing of the Declaration of Independence, the author sweeps back in time to the cave dwellers. From that time to the fall of Rome in 476 A.D., the determination to gain freedom is shown as the spark that encourages great inventions, discoveries, and political movements.

Moccasin Trail **by Eloise Jarvis McGraw, illustrated by Paul Galdone. COWARD.**

A runaway who is clawed by a grizzly and left for dead, Jim is raised by the Crow Indians and becomes a mountain man. Receiving a letter from his little brother asking for help, Jim finds his orphaned family on a wagon train heading to Oregon. He agrees to stay with them on the dangerous journey west. It is Jim's courage and Crow training that help them survive.

Red Sails to Capri by Ann Weil, illustrated by C. B. Falls. VIKING.

Three wealthy strangers come to Michele's small island village and stay at his parents' inn. Their good spirits and desire for adventure soon convince Michele and his friends to help the strangers explore a forbidden cave. Their discovery of the now-famous Blue Grotto changes the lives of everyone on Capri.

Charlotte's Web by E. B. White, illustrated by Garth Williams. HARPER.

After being raised by the farmer's daughter, Wilbur, a pig, is sold to another farm where his companion is a gray spider named Charlotte. When it becomes apparent that Wilbur is being fattened up for slaughtering, Charlotte promises to save him. The words that begin appearing in Charlotte's web amaze the farmer and bring hope to Wilbur.

1952 AWARD

Ginger Pye by Eleanor Estes, illustrated by Louis Slobodkin. HARCOURT BRACE.

The only clue to the mysterious disappearance of Ginger, the Pye family dog, is the unusual man in the mustard-colored hat. Jerry and Rachel look everywhere for their little dog, occasionally seeing the mustard-hatted man, and finally solve the mystery of Ginger's disappearance.

Published in a new edition in 2000 (Harcourt).

HONORS

Americans before Columbus by Elizabeth Baity, illustrated by C. B. Falls. VIKING.

A study of pre-Columbian peoples in the Americas, this book describes their art, architecture, music, literature, and culture from the earliest times to that of Columbus. The text is prefaced with photographs of art and architecture and includes ink drawings in every chapter.

The Apple and the Arrow by Mary and Conrad Buff, illustrated by the authors. HOUGHTON MIFFLIN.

Caught by tyrant Gessler's soldier, Walter's father, William Tell, is forced to either shoot an apple on Walter's head or die. He successfully shoots the apple but is imprisoned. Breaking free, Tell kills Gessler and starts the revolution that wins Switzerland's freedom.

Minn of the Mississippi by Holling Clancy Holling. HOUGHTON MIFFLIN.

Over a twenty-five-year period a snapping turtle makes her way from the source of the Mississippi to the Delta. Along the way she encounters a variety of adventures, lays eggs as she grows older, and introduces readers to the varied people, places, and wildlife along the river.

The Defender by Nicholas Kalashnikoff, illustrated by
Claire and George Louden. SCRIBNER.

In turn-of-the-century Siberia, Turgen, a widowed hunter and herbalist, becomes the target of the local shaman when he begins to protect the shy, fast-disappearing mountain rams. Turgen's only friends are a poor widow, whom he befriends and marries, and her two children.

The Light at Tern Rock by Julia L. Sauer, illustrated by Georges Schreiber. VIKING.

Although Mr. Flagg has promised to get them back to shore by December 15, Aunt Martha and Ronnie suddenly realize that they are stuck at the lonely lighthouse until after Christmas. At first angry and sullen, Ronnie finally joins Aunt Martha in a very special celebration of the holiday.

1951 AWARD

Amos Fortune, Free Man by Elizabeth Yates, illustrated by Nora S. Unwin.
ALADDIN/AMERICAN BOOK.

Captured by slavers, Amos, son of an African king, survives the long ocean voyage only to be sold to a New England Quaker. After years of serving and learning from others, Amos buys his own freedom, sets up his own business, and begins to buy and set free other slaves.

HONORS

Gandhi, Fighter without a Sword by Jeanette Eaton, illustrated by Ralph Ray.
MORROW.

From an upper-class life in India, Gandhi travels to England where he becomes a lawyer. Later he goes to South Africa and becomes involved in fighting for civil liberties. Back in India, Gandhi spends the remainder of his life leading the nonviolent independence movement, which finally brings freedom to India and martyrdom to Gandhi.

Better Known as Johnny Appleseed by Mabel Leigh Hunt, illustrated by
James Daugherty. LIPPINCOTT.

Loved by the settlers and the Indians, John Chapman carves a new name and legend for himself by trekking through the wilderness planting apple trees and helping anyone in need. The few facts known about Chapman are carefully interwoven with the Johnny Appleseed legends.

Abraham Lincoln, Friend of the People by Clara Ingram Judson, illustrated with drawings by Robert Frankenberg and Kodachromes of the Chicago Historical Society Lincoln Dioramas. FOLLETT.

Vividly written and carefully researched, the book portrays the struggles Abraham Lincoln had in learning to read, making a living, and finally entering politics. The difficulties of life on the frontier and the problems leading to the Civil War form the background.

The Story of Appleby Capple by Anne Parrish, illustrated by the author. HARPER.

For his Cousin Clement's ninety-ninth birthday, five-year-old Appleby is determined to give the old man the thing he wants most to see: a zebra butterfly. The boy wanders through the alphabet looking for the butterfly. Ink illustrations work people and objects around all twenty-six letters.

1950 AWARD

The Door in the Wall by Marguerite de Angeli, illustrated by the author. DOUBLEDAY.

Crippled by a strange disease, Robin is ready to give up since he knows he will never be a knight. Then the monks help him to find ways to gain strength and courage and ultimately to play an important role in saving his medieval city.

Published in a new edition with an introduction by Ted de Angeli in 1989 (Doubleday).

HONORS

Tree of Freedom by Rebecca Caudill, illustrated by Dorothy B. Morse. VIKING.

During the American Revolution, the Venable family leaves North Carolina to seek new land and get away from British oppression. Their exciting month-long trek over the mountains to Kentucky starts them on the way to new freedom, symbolized by the apple tree, whose seeds have come with the family all the way from France.

The Blue Cat of Castle Town by Catherine Cate Coblentz, illustrated by Janice Holland. LONGMANS, GREEN.

Born under a blue moon, the little kitten is destined to carry the river's song of beauty, peace, and contentment to the unhappy people of Castle Town, Vermont. They have exchanged beauty for money, no longer making things with honesty and unable to "sing their own songs."

George Washington by Genevieve Foster, illustrated by the author. SCRIBNER.

Filled with interesting excerpts from letters and diaries, this animated portrayal of the first president of the United States tells of George Washington's childhood and his many challenges as surveyor, soldier, commander in chief, and president.

Song of the Pines: A Story of Norwegian Lumbering in Wisconsin **by Walter and Marion Havighurst, illustrated by Richard Floethe. WINSTON.**

An orphan, fifteen-year-old Nils joins the Svendsen family and other Norwegian emigrants as they head toward America in the 1850s. They travel to Wisconsin where they stake out a claim for a farm. Nils, having found work in the lumber camps, creates his own business and future in America.

Kildee House **by Rutherford Montgomery, illustrated by Barbara Cooney. DOUBLEDAY.**

Not used to talking or being around people, Jerome Kildee retires to a small house he builds atop a hill in the redwood forest of northern California. Through the animals he shelters and the young people he meets, Kildee's life and the lives of those he encounters become fuller and richer than he ever imagined.

1949 AWARD

King of the Wind **by Marguerite Henry, illustrated by Wesley Dennis. RAND MCNALLY.**

Sure that the motherless Arabian colt is going to be a great racer, Agba, the Sultan's mute slaveboy, raises the animal and stays with it, even when the horse is sent to France. Times are hard for the two, and they are often treated cruelly, but Agba never gives up his belief in the horse that becomes the ancestor of the great Man o' War.

Published in a new edition in 1990 (Simon & Schuster).

HONORS

Story of the Negro **by Arna Bontemps, illustrated by Raymond Lufkin. KNOPF.**

Beginning with the first slave ship to come to Jamestown, Bontemps celebrates the culture and accomplishments of black people throughout the world: from the cultural heritage of Africa to the artists, leaders, and momentous events that have shaped not only black but world culture as well.

My Father's Dragon **by Ruth Stiles Gannett, illustrated by Ruth Chrisman Gannett. RANDOM HOUSE.**

An old alley cat convinces the narrator's father to rescue a baby dragon being used as a ferry by the animals of faraway Wild Island. With chewing gum, toothpaste, lollipops, and ribbons, the little boy keeps lions and tigers from eating him as he tries to rescue the little dragon.

Seabird **by Holling Clancy Holling. HOUGHTON MIFFLIN.**

To help him while away the hours on the whaling ship, Ezra carves a mascot, Seabird, which becomes his constant companion as he journeys around the world and finally gets his own ship. For four generations Seabird brings companionship and luck to Ezra's family as they sail the sea.

Daughter of the Mountains **by Louise Rankin, illustrated by Kurt Wiese.** VIKING.

When Momo's beloved Lhasa terrier is stolen by a wool trader, the Tibetan girl follows him on a long and dangerous journey that takes her through the mountains into India and finally to Calcutta.

1948 AWARD

The Twenty-one Balloons **by William Pène du Bois, illustrated by the author.** VIKING.

Professor Sherman leaves San Francisco in one hot air balloon and three weeks later is found in the Atlantic Ocean, clinging to the remains of twenty balloons and refusing to tell how he got there.

HONORS

The Quaint and Curious Quest of Johnny Longfoot **by Catherine Besterman, illustrated by Warren Chappell.** BOBBS-MERRILL.

Sent to the country to stay with his very thrifty uncle, Johnny, son of the shoe king, outwits guard dogs and a bear to reach the miserly old man. Not welcome, he goes on a quest that leads him to a cat who sends him to look for gold and seven-league boots. Leading a band of dogs, cats, bears, and his tagalong uncle, Johnny resourcefully succeeds in his mission.

Pancakes-Paris **by Claire Huchet Bishop, illustrated by Georges Schreiber.** VIKING.

Before the war there was heat and food and paper. Now Charles wishes for a way to show his little sister the fun of Mardi Gras and the wonderful crepes they ate. When two American soldiers suddenly enter his life and give him a strange box that they claim holds the ingredients for crepes, things start to happen.

The Cow-tail Switch, and Other West African Stories **by Harold Courlander, illustrated by Madye Lee Chastain.** HOLT.

Puns, trickster tales, creation tales, parables, and proverbs form the basis for these seventeen stories from West Africa. Faithfully retold from original sources, the stories are great fun to read or tell.

Li Lun, Lad of Courage **by Carolyn Treffinger, illustrated by Kurt Wiese.** ABINGDON.

When Li Lun refuses to join his father on his trip out to sea, the man angrily sends the boy up to the top of their mountain to grow rice. Alone on the mountaintop for

120 days, Li Lun, called a coward by his father and the other boys, courageously faces the elements, determined to complete his task.

Misty of Chincoteague **by Marguerite Henry, illustrated by Wesley Dennis.**
RAND MCNALLY.

When Pony Penning Day comes on Chincoteague Island, Maureen and Paul are determined to buy the Phantom and her filly, Misty. They work hard and save $102, and finally the two spirited animals are theirs. Now the children must train the wild ponies to be around people, instead of running wild on Assateague.

1947 AWARD

Miss Hickory **by Carolyn Sherwin Bailey, illustrated by Ruth Gannett.** VIKING.

With an apple twig for a body and a hickory nut for a head, Miss Hickory stubbornly refuses help as she tries to survive a cold New Hampshire winter alone.

HONORS

Wonderful Year **by Nancy Barnes, pseud. (Helen Simmons Adams), illustrated by Kate Seredy.** MESSNER.

Eleven-year-old Ellen and her fun-loving parents move from an easy life in Kansas to a ranch in western Colorado. They enjoy life as they plant trees and build a home and a barn. For Ellen, the best part is her friendship with fifteen-year-old Ronnie and the adventures they share.

Big Tree **by Mary and Conrad Buff, illustrated by the authors.** VIKING.

A glorious tree that can live thousands of years and has no fear of fire or insects, the redwood Wawona begins to grow long before the pyramids and the coming of Christ. Nothing threatens the huge and ancient tree until man arrives with axes and saws. But others recognize his importance and offer protection to the redwood.

The Avion My Uncle Flew **by Cyrus Fisher, pseud. (Darwin L. Teilhet), illustrated by Richard Floethe.** APPLETON.

When John's father returns home after World War II, he decides to take his wife and son to France. There John will have a chance to get his injured leg treated and to see his mother's homeland. John does not want to go, but he has no choice. Once there he becomes involved in a mysterious adventure that takes him to southern France and his glider-building uncle.

The Heavenly Tenants **by William Maxwell, illustrated by Ilonka Karasz.** HARPER.

The night before the Maxwells are to leave for three weeks in Virginia, father takes the children outside and shows them the different constellations that make up the zodiac. When no one comes to care for their animals while they are gone, the signs of the zodiac come to Earth and do it for them.

***The Hidden Treasure of Glaston* by Eleanore Jewett, illustrated by Frederick T. Chapman. VIKING.**

When he is forced to leave the country because of his part in the murder of Thomas à Becket, Sir Hugh de Morville leaves his crippled son in the care of the monks at Glaston. As the boy and a new friend explore the area, they discover treasure left by King Arthur and his court and begin an exciting and suspenseful search for the Holy Grail.

1946 AWARD

***Strawberry Girl* by Lois Lenski, illustrated by the author. LIPPINCOTT.**

Birdie's family wants to make a good living growing strawberries and oranges in turn-of-the-century Florida. Unfortunately their shiftless neighbors, the Slaters, fight them every step of the way.

HONORS

***Justin Morgan Had a Horse* by Marguerite Henry, illustrated by Wesley Dennis. RAND MCNALLY.**

Justin Morgan does not want the little colt that follows him and Joel home. But Joel raises and trains it, and the two soon realize that the little horse is something very special, not to mention very fast. Years later it becomes the first of a new breed: the Justin Morgan horse.

***The Moved-Outers* by Florence Crannell Means, illustrated by Helen Blair. HOUGHTON MIFFLIN.**

After the attack on Pearl Harbor, the Ohara family, who have always thought of themselves as Americans, are suddenly "Japanese." Put into internment camps with only the barest of necessities, Sue and her family try not only to survive but to stay loyal Americans.

***New Found World* by Katherine Shippen, illustrated by C. B. Falls. VIKING.**

A history of Latin America, the book begins with a chapter on the topography and the plant and animal life of the area. Additional chapters discuss the native peoples and their interaction with European explorers and colonists. Well-researched, the book covers aspects of Latin American life and history up to the end of World War II.

Bhimsa, the Dancing Bear by Christine Weston, illustrated by Roger Duvoisin. SCRIBNER.

While aimlessly walking in his Indian garden, David is surprised by the approach of a boy, Gopala, and his tame bear, Bhimsa. He eagerly runs away with the two as they wander through India trying to find a way home for Gopala. Bhimsa's dancing attracts attention everywhere, earning them food and getting them into and out of trouble along the way.

1945 AWARD

Rabbit Hill by Robert Lawson, illustrated by the author. VIKING.

The excitement among the wild creatures is contagious as Little Georgie enthusiastically tells every one of them that new folks are coming to the old farmhouse. All of the animals anxiously await the day the newcomers will arrive, afraid they might be the kind who have guns or dogs or even poison.

HONORS

The Silver Pencil by Alice Dalgliesh, illustrated by Katherine Milhous. SCRIBNER.

After her father's sudden death, Janet and her mother begin a series of moves that take them from Trinidad, to England, to the United States, and then to Nova Scotia. Along the way, Janet holds fast to the silver pencil her father gave her, finding that writing is a solace.

Lone Journey: The Life of Roger Williams by Jeanette Eaton, illustrated by Woodi Ishmael. HARCOURT BRACE.

From childhood onward, Roger Williams is a champion for religious freedom. Again and again he speaks out for separation of church and state, risking his own life and trying to save the lives of others. Finally Williams becomes the founder of the Providence Colony in America, where settlers of all religious faiths can find refuge.

The Hundred Dresses by Eleanor Estes, illustrated by Louis Slobodkin. HARCOURT BRACE.

Wanda Petronski, who speaks in broken English and always wears the same sparkling clean dress to school each day, brags to the other girls that she has a hundred dresses at home. Wanda is laughed at and teased by the other girls, and she and her family move away. Only then do the girls find Wanda's beautifully drawn pictures of one hundred dresses.

Abraham Lincoln's World: 1809–1865 by Genevieve Foster, illustrated by
the author. SCRIBNER.

As Abraham Lincoln grows from birth to death, the things happening throughout
the world affect him and his country. Chapter by chapter the stories of not only
Lincoln but also Napolean, Jefferson, Tecumseh, Jackson, Bismarck, and others are
told alternately to give a full and fascinating picture of world events.

1944 AWARD

Johnny Tremain: A Novel for Old and Young by Esther Forbes, illustrated by
Lynd Ward. HOUGHTON MIFFLIN.

Fourteen-year-old apprentice silversmith Johnny Tremain has a terrible accident that
forces him to give up his work. He becomes involved with Sam Adams and the other
Boston patriots, takes part in the Boston Tea Party, and plays a role in the battle of
Lexington.

*Published in a new edition with illustrations by Michael McCurdy in 1998
(Houghton Mifflin).*

HONORS

Rufus M. by Eleanor Estes, illustrated by Louis Slobodkin. HARCOURT BRACE.

A lively and imaginative little boy, Rufus is the youngest of the four Moffat children.
Anxious to do his part for the war effort, he knits washcloths, plants a victory garden,
and earns enough money selling popcorn to become a Victory Boy.

Fog Magic by Julia L. Sauer, illustrated by Lynd Ward. VIKING.

In every generation of Addingtons there is one person for whom the dense fog of
Nova Scotia is magical. Walking toward the deserted village of Blue Cove on a foggy
day, Greta comes upon a thriving village she has never seen before. It is the Blue Cove
of one hundred years ago.

These Happy Golden Years by Laura Ingalls Wilder, illustrated by Helen Sewell
and Mildred Boyle. HARPER.

Laura Ingalls, though still a student herself, begins teaching in small schools and
sewing to earn tuition money for Mary's education. Whether working hard in town,
teaching, living on her family's claim on the Dakota prairie, or finally deciding to
marry Almanzo, Laura realizes how lucky she is to have her warm, happy family.

Mountain Born by Elizabeth Yates, illustrated by Nora S. Unwin. COWARD.

Nursed back to life by Peter's mother, Biddy, a black lamb, is given to six-year-old
Peter to raise. Bright and brave, Biddy becomes the leader of the herd, repeatedly
alerting her human keepers to impending disaster.

1943 AWARD

Adam of the Road by Elizabeth Janet Gray, illustrated by Robert Lawson. VIKING.

Adam, his minstrel father, their horse, and Adam's trained dog, Nick, are traveling in thirteenth-century England, singing and telling stories for food and a place to sleep. When Nick is stolen, father and son try desperately to find him and become separated from each other.

HONORS

The Middle Moffat by Eleanor Estes, illustrated by Louis Slobodkin. HARCOURT BRACE.

Janey is the "middle Moffat," trying hard to be serious and to do everything well. Things do not seem to work out quite as she plans (her organ recital turns into an escape for thousands of moths), but the little girl is undeterred. She continues to make bold plans with outrageously funny results.

"Have You Seen Tom Thumb?" by Mabel Leigh Hunt, illustrated by Fritz Eichenberg. LIPPINCOTT.

From the age of five, Charles Sherwood Stratton, only twenty-five inches tall and weighing fifteen pounds, is presented to the world by P. T. Barnum as General Tom Thumb. A charming, humorous person, he travels all over the world with Barnum.

1942 AWARD

The Matchlock Gun by Walter Edmonds, illustrated by Paul Lantz. DODD, MEAD.

Edward, his mother, and his little sister have only one defense against the French and the Indians—a huge matchlock gun. When attacked, his mother is wounded, and Edward must use the gun to save their lives.

Published in a new edition in 1989 (Putnam).

HONORS

George Washington's World by Genevieve Foster, illustrated by the author. SCRIBNER.

From birth to death, the story of George Washington's life and the lives of other well-known kings, soldiers, politicians, and scientists of the same period are interwoven. In each section the author skillfully provides a worldview of events.

Down Ryton Water by Eva Roe Gaggin, illustrated by Elmer Hader. VIKING.

Escaping the religious persecution of their English countrymen, Matt and his family and neighbors head down Ryton Water for freedom in Holland. Finally ready to face the long and dangerous voyage to the New World, all of them board the Mayflower and Speedwell to sail to what becomes the Plymouth Colony.

Indian Captive: The Story of Mary Jemison by **Lois Lenski, illustrated by the author.** LIPPINCOTT.

Even though other settlers have been slaughtered by the French and the Indians, Pa refuses to let his family go east to safety. They, too, are captured, and only young, blond-haired Mary survives, forced to become a part of the Seneca people.

Little Town on the Prairie by **Laura Ingalls Wilder, illustrated by Helen Sewell and Mildred Boyle.** HARPER.

Laura is fifteen and, in warm weather, working hard with Ma and Pa on their Dakota Territory claim. She earns what she can to help pay for Mary's courses at the College for the Blind, and, with her family, she spends the long, cold, but friend-filled winters in town.

1941 AWARD

Call It Courage by **Armstrong Sperry, illustrated by the author.** MACMILLAN.

Mocked by the other boys because of his fear of the sea, Mafatu secretly takes a small boat and leaves his village. Alone on a terrifying ocean voyage, the boy, son of a Polynesian chief, overcomes his fear of the sea.

HONORS

Young Mac of Fort Vancouver by **Mary Jane Carr, illustrated by Richard Holberg.** CROWELL.

Traveling west to Fort Vancouver in 1832, Young Mac is determined to become a fur-trading Northman and not a full-fledged member of the white world. Contact with Dr. McLoughlan, head of the fort, and other white and mixed-heritage men causes him to reconsider his decision.

Blue Willow by **Doris Gates, illustrated by Paul Lantz.** VIKING.

With her small family wandering from place to place so that Dad can find work, Janey has never really had a home or school or friends. Maybe the San Joaquin Valley will be the place where everything changes, a place where they can stay and she can finally bring the blue willow plate out for good.

Nansen by **Anna Gertrude Hall, illustrated by Boris Artzybasheff.** VIKING.

Determined to learn as much as he can as a little boy (and even more determined as an adult), Fridtjof Nansen grows to be one of Norway's most famous citizens. He is an explorer who travels all the way to the North Pole, a statesman, and, most difficult of all, a fighter for world peace and a winner of the Nobel Peace Prize.

The Long Winter by Laura Ingalls Wilder, illustrated by Helen Sewell and Mildred Boyle. HARPER.

The Ingalls family, pioneering in the Dakota Territory, stoically endure a dreary succession of blizzards. Huddled in the family store, they and their neighbors must depend upon their ingenuity to prevent freezing and starvation.

1940 AWARD

Daniel Boone by James Daugherty, illustrated by the author. VIKING.

A rugged frontiersman and a leader of pioneers, Daniel Boone starts life in Pennsylvania and ends it eighty-six years later in Missouri, an almost legendary character. Boone's longing for adventure, his bravery, and his foolishness are examined honestly in this biography that sings the praises of pioneer men and women in words and vigorous drawings.

HONORS

Boy with a Pack by Stephen W. Meader, illustrated by Edward Shenton. HARCOURT BRACE.

Bill fills a backpack with things to sell in Ohio and, with two years of savings, leaves his New Hampshire mill town on foot. The 1837 journey is long and hard but filled with all kinds of adventures, danger, and amazing good luck.

Runner of the Mountain Tops: The Life of Louis Agassiz by Mabel Robinson, illustrated by Lynd Ward. RANDOM HOUSE.

A brilliant naturalist and the founder of Harvard's Agassiz Museum, Louis Agassiz is realistically portrayed from his childhood in Switzerland through his years as a Harvard professor. Agassiz's fascination with all of nature and his great teaching ability are evident throughout the book.

The Singing Tree by Kate Seredy, illustrated by the author. VIKING.

Four years after the end of *The Good Master,* the First World War has started, and Mother, Jancsi, and cousin Kate are left to take care of the farm as Father and Uncle Sandor are called to fight. The three of them hold the farm together and make it a refuge for orphans, relatives, and even prisoners of war.

By the Shores of Silver Lake by Laura Ingalls Wilder, illustrated by Helen Sewell and Mildred Boyle. HARPER.

The Ingalls have not had a good crop since the grasshoppers came. Pa decides they will make one more move, this time to Dakota Territory. The family spends a happy winter taking in other settlers and earning money to send Mary, blind from scarlet fever, to a special school.

1939 AWARD

Thimble Summer by Elizabeth Enright, illustrated by the author.
FARRAR & RINEHART.

All kinds of good things seem to happen after Garnet finds the silver thimble in the dried-up river bed. The nine-year-old farm girl notices that the drought finally breaks, she has an exciting time being locked in the public library with a friend, and her pet pig wins a blue ribbon at the fair.

Published in a new edition in 1990 (Henry Holt).

HONORS

Nino by Valenti Angelo, illustrated by the author. VIKING.

While his father works in America to earn their fare to California, Nino and his mother stay with his grandfather in his small Italian village. The little boy and his family and friends share holidays, trips to the city, and small but exciting adventures that create a memorable picture of turn-of-the-century Italy.

Mr. Popper's Penguins by Richard and Florence Atwater, illustrated by Robert Lawson. LITTLE, BROWN.

From the moment he is given a penguin as a pet, Mr. Popper's life starts changing. He converts his basement into an ice rink, finds a friend for his lonely bird, and suddenly has twelve penguins to feed instead of one.

"Hello the Boat!" by Phyllis Crawford, illustrated by Edward Laning. HOLT.

The entire Doak family pitches in to get their store-boat from Pittsburgh to Cincinnati in 1817. Along the Ohio River, settlers shout out, "Hello the boat!" and the family eagerly pushes the boat ashore and enthusiastically opens the store. On their way, the Doaks encounter thieves, learn about the history of the river area, and have a surprisingly good time.

Leader by Destiny: George Washington, Man and Patriot by Jeanette Eaton, illustrated by Jack Manley Rose. HARCOURT.

Not a man who plans what he wants but rather one who allows things to shape him and his future, George Washington lives a life full of adventure and responsibility as he grows up. The fifty-two years of his life that Eaton covers contain much of the history and many of the famous people of his time.

Penn by Elizabeth Janet Gray, illustrated by George Gillett Whitney. VIKING.

Until he converts to the Quaker religion, William Penn leads a privileged upper-class life. Then he loses everything and is imprisoned. After fighting hard for religious freedom, Penn is allowed to go to America and found the new colony of Pennsylvania, based on the principles for which he fought.

1938 AWARD

The White Stag by Kate Seredy, illustrated by the author. VIKING.

Based on legends about the founding of Hungary, this stirring story begins with Nimrod receiving a prophesy from God. He tells his people to follow the White Stag and Nimrod's sons to the west. During their long and dangerous journey, the people move valiantly westward until the birth of Attila, who one day leads them heroically into what becomes Hungary.

HONORS

Pecos Bill by James Cloyd Bowman, illustrated by Laura Bannon. LITTLE, BROWN.

Raised by coyotes and able to speak to animals, Pecos Bill reluctantly accepts the knowledge that he is one of those dreaded inhuman humans. He becomes a cowboy and does things in legendary proportion: busting up a cyclone, breaking up a cattle rustling gang, and rounding up 39,000,000 cattle and driving them to market.

Bright Island by Mabel Robinson, illustrated by Lynd Ward. RANDOM HOUSE.

Strong, independent, and committed to life on her family's small island off the coast of Maine, Thankful very reluctantly agrees to attend school on the mainland. There, life is so foreign that she initially feels like a total outsider among the other high school students.

On the Banks of Plum Creek by Laura Ingalls Wilder, illustrated by Helen Sewell and Mildred Boyle. HARPER.

After finally reaching Minnesota and planting a wheat crop, the Ingalls lose it to a horde of grasshoppers. Determined to stay, Pa goes to work for other farmers. Laura goes to school, shares adventures with friends, but most of all enjoys the moments when her family is together and Pa is back playing the fiddle.

1937 AWARD

Roller Skates by Ruth Sawyer, illustrated by Valenti Angelo. VIKING.

Her wealthy parents in Europe, Lucinda spends a glorious year living with two teachers, skating all over New York City, and making friends everywhere. The people she meets, whether it is her impoverished musician neighbor or the hansom cab driver, appreciate her energy, friendliness, and determination.

HONORS

The Golden Basket by Ludwig Bemelmans, illustrated by the author. VIKING.

A staid English father and his two little daughters visit Bruges, Belgium, and stay at the Golden Basket Hotel. The girls and the hotel owner's son enjoy exploring the famous city. While visiting a cathedral, they meet twelve little girls standing in two straight lines, the youngest and spunkiest being Madeline.

Winterbound by Margery Bianco, illustrated by Kate Seredy. VIKING.

With both of their parents gone for months, nineteen-year-old Kay and sixteen-year-old Garry take on managing both the rented cottage and their younger brother and sister. During a long, cold, but very exciting Depression-era winter, they make friends, earn and save money, and gain strength and independence.

The Codfish Musket by Agnes Hewes, illustrated by Armstrong Sperry. DOUBLEDAY.

Even as a youngster, Dan has a keen eye for fine rifles and arms. On a mission to Washington for his Boston employer, Dan becomes secretary to Thomas Jefferson. The president sends him into the frontier with a message for Merriwether Lewis, but along the way Dan spots gun thieves arming the Indians. He defeats them and delivers his message, finally returning to Washington.

Whistler's Van by Idwal Jones, illustrated by Zhenya Gay. VIKING.

After his grandfather disappears one night with a cart and pony, Gwilyn decides he wants a chance to wander through Wales as well. When the Ringos, a family of gypsies, appear at the farmhouse and whistle, Gwilyn goes off with them for a summer full of music, adventure, and, most important, horses.

Phebe Fairchild: Her Book by Lois Lenski, illustrated by the author. STOKES.

When Phebe's mother decides to join Phebe's father on a sea voyage, the ten-year-old is sent to stay with relatives in the country. Life in 1830 rural Connecticut at first seems rigid to Phebe, and her copy of *Mother Goose* is a constant source of support. The child comes to appreciate her relatives, their simple life, their generosity, and their sense of fun.

Audubon by Constance Rourke, illustrated by James MacDonald, with 12 colored plates from original Audubon prints. HARCOURT BRACE.

Despite mysterious beginnings, John James Audubon manages to leave France and go to America. He marries but continues to traipse the countryside in search of birds and small animals to paint. Carefully researched, the book offers a well-rounded look at the man who became known for his nineteenth-century paintings of American birds.

1936 AWARD

Caddie Woodlawn by Carol Ryrie Brink, illustrated by Kate Seredy. MACMILLAN.

Eleven years old in 1864, Caddie roams the woods and rivers of western Wisconsin with her brothers as her mother relentlessly tries to make her into a young "lady." The mischievous redhead's adventures with Indians and pioneers are full of fun and excitement.

Published in a new edition with illustrations by Trina Schart Hyman in 1973 (Simon & Schuster).

HONORS

Young Walter Scott by Elizabeth Janet Gray, illustrated by Kate Seredy. VIKING.

Despite years of living with country relatives, Walter is determined not to let his lame leg stand in his way once he is at home again. This lively, fictionalized biography transports readers to late eighteenth-century Edinburgh, Scotland, and offers an engrossing introduction to the life of the famous novelist.

The Good Master by Kate Seredy, illustrated by the author. VIKING.

Jancsi is fascinated by his city cousin Kate's daring and reckless behavior. Whether she is stopping a stampede of horses, nearly drowning in the river, or running off with gypsies, she is a marvel and a delight to the Hungarian country folk.

All Sail Set: A Romance of the Flying Cloud by Armstrong Sperry. WINSTON.

Fifteen-year-old Thach goes to work for the great Donald McKay making drawings of his plans for the clipper ship *Flying Cloud*. The ship completed, Thach becomes an apprentice, sails around the Horn, is initiated by "Neptune," contends with mutineers, and nearly loses his life in a shipboard fire.

Honk, the Moose by Phil Stong, illustrated by Kurt Wiese. DODD, MEAD.

The temperature is thirty below zero and the snow is seven feet deep when the boys find a moose in Ivar's father's stable. The town is in an uproar as everyone tries to think of ways to get the gentle and very funny beast to leave.

1935 AWARD

Dobry by Monica Shannon, illustrated by Atanas Katchamakoff. VIKING.

Bulgarian peasant boy Dobry tries to convince his mother that he must be an artist. He does not want to plow the fields as his ancestors did. Dobry's grandfather understands, but until Dobry sculpts a beautiful nativity scene in the snow to prove his talents, his mother is not convinced.

HONORS

Davy Crockett by Constance Rourke, illustrated by James MacDonald. HARCOURT BRACE.

Davy Crockett is a bigger-than-life character: he is a pioneer, hunter, teller of tales, soldier, statesman, and legendary American hero. Rourke writes a well-researched and well-documented biography filled with anecdotes and comments by Crockett and his contemporaries.

Pageant of Chinese History by Elizabeth Seeger, illustrated by Bernard Watkins. LONGMANS, GREEN.

Using a conversational style, Seeger leads the reader through Chinese history starting with mythical and legendary times. Then she writes about each of the dynasties, ending with the Manchu in 1912 and the beginning of the republic. Political and cultural history are the focus of most of the book.

A Day on Skates: The Story of a Dutch Picnic by Hilda Van Stockum, illustrated by the author. HARPER.

The canals of Holland are finally frozen solid, and the headmaster has a surprise. He takes the children on an all-day skating picnic. In spite of a few accidents, it is a thoroughly enjoyable time. Many black-and-white drawings and eight full-color illustrations show the festive atmosphere of the day.

1934 AWARD

Invincible Louisa: The Story of the Author of Little Women by Cornelia Meigs. LITTLE, BROWN.

The life of Louisa May Alcott is chronicled through her lively involvement with family and friends. Incidents reveal that her invincible spirit keeps the family afloat during the darkest of times and always keeps them happy. Family photographs and a chronology are included.

Published in a new edition with an introduction by the author in 1968 (Little, Brown).

HONORS

The Winged Girl of Knossos by Erick Berry, pseud. (Allena Best), illustrated by the author. APPLETON.

Spirited, athletic, and beautiful Inas, daughter of Daidalos, helps her father with his flying experiments on the Isle of Crete during the time of King Minos. Having to leave Crete hurriedly, she does so by flying out on a glider built by her father.

The Big Tree of Bunlahy: Stories of My Own Countryside by Padraic Colum, illustrated by Jack Yeats. MACMILLAN.

Twelve fine old Irish tales and one original one are woven together by the storyteller who introduces each story. All are said to have been heard under the Tree of Bunlahy, the great elm tree with big, smooth stones under it. There the villagers would sit and listen to these tales of animals, heroes, and leprechans.

The ABC Bunny by Wanda Gág, illustrated by the author; hand lettered by Howard Gág. COWARD.

Lithographs filled with curved lines show a bunny romping through his day. After being scared out of his bed by a crashing apple, the bunny meets many animals. Each large, bright red letter of the alphabet is accompanied by a text that carries the ABC lesson along in a rhythmic manner. The song, with words and music, is included.

Glory of the Seas by Agnes Hewes, illustrated by N. C. Wyeth. KNOPF.

The exciting early days of the clipper ships, the controversial Fugitive Slave Law, and the inner conflict caused by civil disobedience are at the center of this story set in Boston in the 1850s. When the *Flying Cloud* sails to San Francisco in just eighty-nine days, many Bostonians dream of sailing to California.

The Apprentice of Florence by Anne Kyle, illustrated by Erick Berry, pseud. (Allena Best). HOUGHTON MIFFLIN.

Nemo, a sixteen-year-old Florentine apprentice, is sent to Constantinople on business in 1453. The city is besieged by Turks, and Nemo is hurt. On his return, young Christopher Columbus tells him that his father, thought to be dead, is alive. More adventures ensue as Nemo searches for his lost father.

New Land by Sarah Schmidt, illustrated by Frank Dobias. MCBRIDE.

It is the 1930s when Dad, the seventeen-year-old twins, and their younger sister arrive in Wyoming to homestead on an unproved claim. Rivalries on the football field and in the new vocational school, a blinding snowstorm, and troubles with the "big man" are overcome, and a new home is established.

Swords of Steel by Elsie Singmaster, illustrated by David Hendrickson. HOUGHTON MIFFLIN.

Although he has heard talk of the differences between the North and the South, it is not until 1859, when his beloved, free black friend is kidnapped to be sold, that John feels personal involvement in the conflict. In six years John grows from childhood to manhood with the Civil War intruding on and then enveloping his life.

The Forgotten Daughter by Caroline Dale Snedeker, illustrated by Dorothy P. Lathrop. DOUBLEDAY.

When his wife dies in childbirth while he is traveling, the Roman centurion is told that both mother and child are dead. His daughter is subjected to the hardships of second-century life as a slave. Eventually she falls in love with a high-born Roman, and the plague unites her with her father.

1933 AWARD

Young Fu of the Upper Yangtze by **Elizabeth Foreman Lewis, illustrated by Kurt Wiese. WINSTON.**

The empress has died and political life is in turmoil when Young Fu and his mother move from their village to Chungking so that he can be apprenticed to a coppersmith. Young Fu must constantly use his wits to protect his mother and himself from thieves and rascals.

Published in a new edition with an introduction by Pearl S. Buck and illustrations by Ed Young in 1973 (Holt Rinehart & Winston). Published in a new edition with a foreword by Katherine Paterson, notes by Daniel J. Meissner, and illustrations by William Low in 2007 (Henry Holt).

HONORS

Children of the Soil: A Story of Scandinavia by **Nora Burglon, illustrated by Edgar Parin d'Aulaire. DOUBLEDAY.**

Two very poor but ambitious and industrious children live with their mother in Sweden at the turn of the twentieth century. The soil they hoe is poor, their crab trap washes out to sea, and a weaving contest is lost to the gentry. With a little help from a Tomte and a lot of work on their part, they acquire some livestock and the promise of a happier future.

Swift Rivers by **Cornelia Meigs, illustrated by Forrest W. Orr. LITTLE, BROWN.**

When his mean-spirited uncle locks him out of the house where he was raised, Chris knows it is time to become a man. The harsh 1835 Wisconsin winter and the bountiful woods lead him to try floating logs down to St. Louis. As a part of the early days of the logging industry, Chris has many adventures on the river.

The Railroad to Freedom: A Story of the Civil War by **Hildegarde Swift, illustrated by James Daugherty. HARCOURT BRACE.**

Harriet Tubman, a slave, escapes from the South but goes back again and again, leading three hundred other slaves North to freedom via the dangerous Underground Railroad. The horrifying yet often thrilling adventures are based on incidents from Tubman's life.

1932 AWARD

Waterless Mountain by Laura Adams Armer, illustrated by
Sidney and Laura Adams Armer. LONGMANS, GREEN.

Destined to become a medicine man, introspective Younger Brother learns the songs
and stories of the Navajo Indians and begins to create songs of his own. Skillfully
interwoven into the story are the early twentieth-century culture and heritage of the
tribe.

HONORS

Jane's Island by Marjorie Allee, illustrated by Maitland de Gorgoza. HOUGHTON
MIFFLIN.

Ellen, a college freshman, spends the summer with twelve-year-old Jane in Woods
Hole, Massachusetts, where Jane's father is a marine biologist. The girls enjoy light
summer adventures while fishing and picnicking. Jane is a competent naturalist who
imparts a good measure of scientific information throughout the story.

Truce of the Wolf and Other Tales of Old Italy by Mary Gould Davis, illustrated by
Jay Van Everen. HARCOURT BRACE.

Seven widely varied Italian stories tell of such things as Saint Francis taming a men-
acing wolf, of an obstinate and heroic donkey, and of how a street in Florence was
named. The tales, all told with a bit of Italian folk humor, come from many sources,
including a Tuscan peasant woman and *The Decameron.*

Calico Bush by Rachel Field, illustrated by Allen Lewis. MACMILLAN.

In 1743, twelve-year-old Marguerite is bound out to a family in Maine. Discriminated
against by the parents because she is French, she finds happiness with the children as
they all face hardships and the rigors of life in the Maine wilderness.

The Fairy Circus by Dorothy P. Lathrop, illustrated by the author. MACMILLAN.

When the circus tent goes up, it is so big that it encloses the places where the fairies live. They all scramble for the best view, and when it is over they decide to have a
circus of their own. The fairies and woodland animals use grand imaginations as they
re-create the circus in their own way.

Out of the Flame by Eloise Lownsbery, illustrated by Elizabeth Tyler Wolcott.
LONGMANS, GREEN.

In the sixteenth century, Pierre is first a page then a squire as he becomes trained to
be a knight in the court of Francis I. He attends tournaments, visits with great intel-
lectuals, and learns music and botany with the royal children. Before the story ends,
he and the children are abducted and released by pirates.

Boy of the South Seas by Eunice Tietjens, illustrated by Myrtle Sheldon. COWARD.

When a ship arrives in the harbor of the Marquesas Islands, young Teiki's curiosity gets ahold of him, and he climbs aboard and falls asleep. He awakens when the vessel is under sail and there is no turning back. At the island of Moorea, he swims ashore and makes a new life for himself.

1931 AWARD

The Cat Who Went to Heaven by Elizabeth Coatsworth, illustrated by Lynd Ward. MACMILLAN.

A starving Japanese artist is commissioned to paint the death of Buddha. He longs to include his gentle cat, Good Fortune, among the animals, but legend says cats cannot enter heaven. Because of her goodness, he paints her, and the little animal dies of happiness. When the priest objects, the painting miraculously changes to show Buddha accepting the cat.

Published in a new edition with new illustrations by Lynd Ward in 1958 (Macmillan).

HONORS

Mountains Are Free by Julia Davis Adams, illustrated by
Theodore Nadejen. DUTTON.

Bruno, a young Swiss orphan who is being raised by the Tells, suddenly decides to become a page to an Austrian, saying he will return when he can earn his own way. The stirring of democracy causes conflicts as the Swiss try to rebel against the harshness of their Habsburg rulers.

Garram the Hunter: A Boy of the Hill Tribes by Herbert Best, illustrated by
Erick Berry, pseud. (Allena Best). DOUBLEDAY.

Hoping to find an ally for his chieftain father, Garram is sent to stay with the emir and becomes a favorite of the ruler. When he returns home, he discovers not only a plot to imprison his father but receives word that the eastern tribes are threatening.

Meggy MacIntosh by Elizabeth Janet Gray, illustrated by Marguerite de Angeli.
DOUBLEDAY.

In 1775 orphaned fifteen-year-old Meggy leaves her native Scotland to sail for the colony of North Carolina. There she joins Flora MacDonald, who had helped Bonnie Prince Charlie escape. Meggy becomes involved in the revolutionary cause and moves away from Flora, a loyalist.

Spice and the Devil's Cave by Agnes Hewes, illustrated by Lynd Ward. KNOPF.

At a workshop in Portugal, Bartholomew Diaz, Vasco da Gama, and Ferdinand Magellan gather to discuss their theory that an all-sea route around the Cape of

Good Hope, also known as the Devil's Cave, must exist. The theft by pirates of the only known maps adds interest and intrigue.

Queer Person **by Ralph Hubbard, illustrated by Harold von Schmidt. DOUBLEDAY.**

He can neither hear nor talk, and at age four he wanders into a camp of Pikuni Indians. His silence earns him the name Queer Person, and he is raised by an old woman in the tribe. During his test of bravery, he rescues the chief's lost son from the Crows, and it is revealed that they are brothers.

Ood-Le-Uk the Wanderer **by Alice Lide and Margaret Johansen, illustrated by Raymond Lufkin. LITTLE, BROWN.**

An Alaskan Eskimo caught on an ice floe crosses the Bering Straight. After years of wandering, he returns home to establish trade between his tribe and the Siberian tribesmen. Once known as a weakling, after his hazardous adventures he is known to be a brave man.

The Dark Star of Itzá: The Story of a Pagan Princess **by Alida Malkus, illustrated by Lowell Houser. HARCOURT BRACE.**

When the khan of Chichén Itzá kidnaps the betrothed of another Mayan chieftain, war breaks out, and the city falls into the hands of the Toltecs. The seventeen-year-old daughter of Chichén Itzá's chief priest agrees to be the sacrifice that will save her city, but her father bravely finds a way to save her.

Floating Island **by Anne Parrish, illustrated by the author. HARPER.**

All packed up and on board a ship bound for the tropics, a doll family and their doll house land on Floating Island after their ship wrecks. They adapt well to the island but soon realize that dolls can never be happy if they are away from children for too long. They then arrange their own rescue.

1930 AWARD

Hitty, Her First Hundred Years **by Rachel Field, illustrated by Dorothy P. Lathrop. MACMILLAN.**

Carved from a block of mountain ash a hundred years before, the six-and-a-half-inch doll now sits secure in the antique shop window and writes her memoirs. She recounts the adventures she had with many different people in places around the world. Illustrations show Hitty in many styles of clothing in her life thus far.

HONORS

Vaino by Julia Davis Adams, illustrated by Lempi Ostman. DUTTON.

Ancient legends of Finland, the lives of three children, and the Finnish Revolution of 1917 are blended together to tell a story filled with strong patriotic spirit. Vaino and his older brother and sister become a part of the revolution that finally frees Finland of foreign domination.

A Daughter of the Seine: The Life of Madame Roland by Jeanette Eaton. HARPER.

Madame Roland's life coincides with the French Revolution. The historical biography describes the childhood, married life, and tragic execution by guillotine of this remarkable woman. Madame Roland is intelligent and strongly supports the revolution, and her salon is depicted as the headquarters of much political activity.

The Jumping-Off Place by Marian Hurd McNeely, illustrated by William Siegel. LONGMANS, GREEN.

When the uncle who cared for them dies, four children pull up stakes in Wisconsin and move to South Dakota. There they weather adventures, hardships, and squatters for the fourteen months it takes to make homesteaders owners of the land.

Pran of Albania by Elizabeth Miller, illustrated by Maud and Miska Petersham. DOUBLEDAY.

In post–World War I Albania amidst a threat of attack from Slavs, fourteen-year-old Pran falls in love. Rather than submit to an arranged marriage, she vows to never marry. After a truce is made, Pran realizes the man she loves is the same man her parents had arranged for her to marry.

Little Blacknose by Hildegarde Swift, illustrated by Lynd Ward. HARCOURT BRACE.

Little Blacknose is none other than the DeWitt Clinton Engine, the first locomotive built for the New York Central Railway. The personified engine tells of his life until he becomes enthroned in New York's Grand Central Terminal.

The Tangle-Coated Horse and Other Tales by Ella Young, illustrated by Vera Bock. LONGMANS, GREEN.

The Fionn Saga, the stories of Finn McCool known in every Gaelic-speaking part of Scotland and all over Ireland, is retold with vigor. The stories begin when McCool is a small boy learning about his heritage and his crafts and end three hundred years later when his son returns from the country of the Ever-Young.

1929 AWARD

The Trumpeter of Krakow: A Tale of the Fifteenth Century by Eric P. Kelly,
illustrated by Angela Pruszynska. MACMILLAN.

For two hundred years the Charnetski family has guarded Poland's most famous
jewel. When the czar of Russia finds out about the valuable crystal, he sends men to
steal it before the Charnetskis can get it to the king of Poland. Adventure, mystery,
and self-sacrifice fill this medieval story set in Krakow.

*Published in a new edition with an introduction by Louise Seaman Bechtel and illustra-
tions by Janina Domanska in 1966 (Simon & Schuster).*

HONORS

The Pigtail of Ah Lee Ben Loo by John Bennett, illustrated by the author.
LONGMANS, GREEN.

Many original stories in prose and verse, and one brief wordless story, are illustrated
with two hundred intriguing and often funny silhouettes. The stories are filled with
robust and irreverent humor: King Arthur's Sir Launcelot is called "Sir Launcelot de
Id-i-otte"! Most of the stories first appeared in *St. Nicholas Magazine*.

Millions of Cats by Wanda Gág, illustrated by the author. COWARD.

A lonely old couple decides to get a cat. Searching for the prettiest one out of a whole
hillside filled with cats, the man comes home with "hundreds of cats, thousands of
cats, millions and billions and trillions of cats." When the cats fight about who is
prettiest, only one is left.

The Boy Who Was by Grace Hallock, illustrated by Harrie Wood. DUTTON.

In 1927 Nino the goatherd shows an artist the wooden figures he has carved of famous
Mediterranean people and proceeds to tell their stories, covering more than 3,000 years
of history. He begins with tales of Odysseus, Pompeii, and the Crusades and then goes
through the nineteenth century, occasionally including himself in the stories.

Clearing Weather by Cornelia Meigs, illustrated by Frank Dobias.
LITTLE, BROWN.

It is just after the American Revolution and the economy has not recovered. When
young Nicholas Drury takes over his family's shipbuilding business, he struggles hard
until the family fortune reverses itself with the successful design, construction, and
voyage of the *Jocasta*, a forerunner of the clipper ship.

The Runaway Papoose by Grace Moon, illustrated by Carl Moon. DOUBLEDAY.

Little Nah-tee runs away when outlaw Indians attack her family's camp. Her parents
cannot find her and move on with the others. Nah-tee and a young shepherd boy she
meets have many adventures as they cross the mesa in search of her parents.

Tod of the Fens by Elinor Whitney, illustrated by Warwick Goble. MACMILLAN.

Fifteenth-century Boston, England, is the setting for the amusing tale of Tod, who lives with a band of men just outside of town. Prince Hal, later to become Henry V, roves about the town in various disguises. Tod, realizing what is happening, tells no one and plays along with the game that is afoot.

1928 AWARD

Gay-Neck, the Story of a Pigeon by Dhan Gopal Mukerji, illustrated by Boris Artzybasheff. DUTTON.

Born in Calcutta, Gay-Neck has thrilling adventures, first traveling all over India and later working as a carrier pigeon for the Indian Army in France during World War I. Eventually he returns to his young owner in India. Sometimes the story is told by Mukerji and at other times by Gay-Neck the pigeon.

HONORS

Downright Dencey by Caroline Dale Snedeker, illustrated by Maginel Wright Barney. DOUBLEDAY.

A Nantucket Quaker community during the War of 1812 provides the background for the story of a young girl named Dencey who first becomes involved with outcast Sammie when she hurls a stone at him. Ashamed, she tries to make amends but Sammie's trust must be won, and that is not easy for Dencey.

The Wonder Smith and His Son: A Tale from the Golden Childhood of the World, retold by Ella Young, illustrated by Boris Artzybasheff. LONGMANS, GREEN.

Fourteen stories of Gubbaun Saor, a mythological creature of Ireland, have been re-told from tales the author heard from English and Gaelic storytellers. The stories capture the lilting cadence of the Irish language and are enhanced by the graphics.

1927 AWARD

Smoky, the Cowhorse by Will James, illustrated by the author. SCRIBNER.

Born free on the open range, Smoky roams the hills until he is caught and gentled by Clint, a cowboy. Stolen and cruelly treated, Smoky kills his captor and runs as an outlaw. Captured again, he becomes a rodeo horse until once more he meets up with Clint and lives out his life on the range where he was born.

Published in a new edition with color illustrations in 1929 (Scribner). Published in a new edition in 2000 (Mountain Press).

HONOR

No record.

1926 AWARD

Shen of the Sea: A Book for Children by Arthur Bowie Chrisman, illustrated by Else Hasselriis. DUTTON.

Sixteen charming and funny original stories are told in traditional folktale style. Most of the stories explain the origins of things like printing, chopsticks, and gunpowder. In several stories, the main character, always reacting the opposite of what is expected, is tricked by the smarter, minor characters.

Published in a new edition in 1968 (Dutton).

HONOR

The Voyagers: Being Legends and Romances of Atlantic Discovery by Padraic Colum, illustrated by Wildred Jones. MACMILLAN.

Convinced that there is another land far away, Portugal's Prince Henry the Navigator gathers together all those who might know anything about it. In a high tower that overlooks the Atlantic Ocean, stories of legends and voyages are told along with those of the discoveries of Columbus and Ponce de León.

1925 AWARD

Tales from Silver Lands by Charles Finger, illustrated by Paul Honoré. DOUBLEDAY.

Nineteen stories that Finger gathered from South American Indian villagers are retold retaining their original flavor. Included are captivating tales of witches, giants, and strange enchantments.

HONORS

Nicholas: A Manhattan Christmas Story by Anne Carroll Moore, illustrated by Jay Van Everen. PUTNAM.

Nicholas, eight inches high, is a little boy from Holland who visits New York City for a few months in the 1920s. While there, he attends parties, visits famous landmarks, and learns about the Dutch influence on the city. His first party is at the library, where he is introduced to many book characters.

The Dream Coach by Anne Parrish and Dillwyn Parrish, illustrated by the authors. MACMILLAN.

The Dream Coach is pulled by one hundred misty horses. Helped by little angels, it travels the night sky dispensing dreams. Four children are introduced in turn, and their fairy-tale-like dreams, often involving inanimate objects that come to life, are shared.

1924 AWARD

The Dark Frigate by Charles Hawes, illustrated by A. L. Ripley. LITTLE, BROWN.

A seagoing adventure turns sour when the *Rose of Devon* is seized in mid-ocean by pirates. The vile, ruthless men force nineteen-year-old Philip to be a part of the pirate crew, and the hangman awaits his return to England. Set in the time of King Charles, the story does not romanticize piracy.

Published in a new edition with a color frontispiece by Anton Otto Fischer in 1934 (Little, Brown). Published in a new edition with an introduction by Lloyd Alexander in 1971 (Little, Brown).

HONOR

No record.

1923 AWARD

The Voyages of Doctor Dolittle by Hugh Lofting, illustrated by the author. STOKES.

Fun and nonsense reign as Dr. John Dolittle, a medical doctor and naturalist who has the ability to talk to animals, sets sail for Spider Monkey Island. There he unites two tribes, becomes king, and sails home inside the 70,000-year-old great glass sea snail. The story is told by the doctor's nine-and-a-half-year-old assistant.

Published in a new edition with slightly revised text, an introduction by Patricia C. and Fredrick L. McKissack, and new illustrations by Michael Hague in 2001 (Books of Wonder/ HarperCollins).

HONOR

No record.

1922 AWARD

The Story of Mankind by Hendrik Willem van Loon, illustrated by the author.
BONI & LIVERIGHT.

Speaking directly to the reader, the author provides a fascinating picture of history from cave peoples to the present (1920). Ideas, movements, and people are more important than dates, and history is shown as something that builds upon itself.

Published with new text in 1926 (Boni & Liveright). Published with new text in 1939 (Pocket Books). Published with new text by Gerard Willem van Loon in 1951 (Liveright). Published with new text by Edwin C. Broome in 1967 (Liveright). Published with new text by an uncredited author in 1972 (Liveright). Published with new text by John Merriman and new illustrations by Adam Simon in 1984 (Liveright). Published with new text by John Merriman and new illustrations by Dirk van Loon in 1999 (Liveright).

HONORS

The Old Tobacco Shop: A True Account of What Befell a Little Boy in Search of Adventure by William Bowen, illustrated by Reginald Birch. MACMILLAN.

Fred is befriended by the hunchback who runs the tobacco shop. Warned never to smoke the magic tobacco in the porcelain jar shaped like a "Chinaman's head," Fred stays away from it for a long time. One day he falters and suddenly finds himself involved in high adventure on the Spanish Main.

The Golden Fleece and the Heroes Who Lived before Achilles by Padraic Colum, illustrated by Willy Pogany. MACMILLAN.

The ancient triumphs and tragedies of the Greek myths are woven through the central story of Jason and his quest for the Golden Fleece. The many stories told by Orpheus to the sailors in the story might be the very ones that the Argonauts heard on their long voyage.

The Great Quest by Charles Hawes, illustrated by George Varian. LITTLE, BROWN.

Twelve-year-old Josiah tells of how his Uncle Seth is tricked by an old friend into selling his shop and buying a ship. Thinking they are going in search of gold, Josiah and his uncle find themselves unwillingly involved in the slave trade and at odds with the crew.

Cedric the Forester by Bernard Marshall, illustrated by J. Scott Williams.
APPLETON.

Cedric, son of a thirteenth-century forester, saves Sir Richard's son and is made his squire. Taught to read and fight, Cedric becomes the best crossbowman in England, and, at the Battle of the Eagles, he is knighted.

The Windy Hill by Cornelia Meigs, illustrated by Elmer and Berta Hader. MACMILLAN.

A brother and sister visit their older cousin in New England. Their cousin was once jovial but is now mysteriously irritable and preoccupied. A chance meeting with the beeman leads to their hearing stories about their own family's history. As they listen, the two children start to understand the cause of their cousin's anxiety.

The
Caldecott
Awards

2015–1938

2015 Caldecott Award

The Adventures of Beekle: The Unimaginary Friend

By Dan Santat

Illustrated by the author

Little, Brown/Hachette

Pencil, crayon, watercolor, ink, and Adobe Photoshop

In four delightful "visual chapters," Beekle, an imaginary friend, undergoes an emotional journey looking for his human. Santat uses fine details, kaleidoscopic saturated colors, and exquisite curved and angular lines to masterfully convey the emotional essence of this special childhood relationship.

"Santat makes the unimaginable, imaginable," said Caldecott Medal Committee Chair Junko Yokota.

ABOUT THE ILLUSTRATOR

Author and illustrator **Dan Santat** has worked on numerous picture books, chapter books, and the graphic novel *Sidekicks,* featuring Captain Amazing. He is a winner of the Silver Medal from the Society of Illustrators for *Oh No! (Or How My Science Project Destroyed the World),* written by Mac Barnett. Santat also is the creator of Disney Channel's hit animated series, *The Replacements.* He graduated with honors from the Art Center College of Design in Pasadena, California, and lives in Southern California with his wife, two children, and various pets.

2015 CALDECOTT HONOR BOOKS

Nana in the City
By Lauren Castillo

Illustrated by the author

CLARION/HOUGHTON MIFFLIN HARCOURT

Watercolor

Castillo's evocative watercolor illustrations tell the story of a young boy's visit to his grandmother, and the reassuring way she helps him to lose his fear and experience the busy, loud city in a new way.

The Noisy Paint Box: The Colors and Sounds of Kandinsky's Abstract Art
By Barb Rosenstock

Illustrated by Mary GrandPré

ALFRED A. KNOPF/RANDOM HOUSE CHILDREN'S BOOKS

Acrylic paint, paper collage

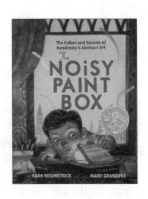

Abstract artist Vasily Kandinsky experienced colors as sounds and sounds as colors; he created work that was bold and groundbreaking using colors from his "noisy paint box." His process is reflected beautifully by Grand-Pré, whose paint flows across the page in ethereal ribbons of color.

Sam & Dave Dig a Hole
By Mac Barnett

Illustrated by Jon Klassen

CANDLEWICK

Colored pencil, digital manipulation

Klassen's use of texture, shape, and earth tones in this deceptively simple book invite readers into the experience of two boys, who, accompanied by their dog, set out to dig a hole. Readers will find an unexpected treasure and be challenged to ponder the meaning of "spectacular."

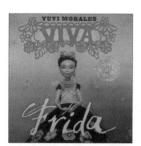

Viva Frida
By Yuyi Morales

Illustrated by the author

ROARING BROOK/NEAL PORTER

Steel, polymer clay, and wool (for stop-motion puppets), and acrylic paint, photography, and digital manipulation

Using a unique variety of media—puppetry, printmaking, painting, and photography—combined with an intoxicating use of color and unfailing sense of composition, Morales celebrates the artistic process.

The Right Word: Roget and His Thesaurus
By Jen Bryant

Illustrated by Melissa Sweet

EERDMANS BOOKS FOR YOUNG READERS

Watercolor, collage, mixed media

Sweet's inspired mixed media illustrations illuminate the personality and work of a man passionately interested in many things. Her collages combine disparate elements to create a cohesive whole, echoing the ways in which Roget ordered the world into lists that evolved into his groundbreaking thesaurus.

This One Summer
By Mariko Tamaki

Illustrated by Jillian Tamaki

FIRST SECOND

Brush pen, Adobe Photoshop

Intricately detailed illustrations in shades of indigo are masterfully layered with the text in this graphic novel. The pacing and strong imagery evoke myriad emotions and ground this poignant and painfully realistic coming-of-age story.

The Caldecott Awards section that follows includes information about the art media used in Caldecott picture books. Each Caldecott title's listing includes the media used to create the book's pictures.

In compiling the media data, no information was regarded as final unless it was found in two independent secondary sources (review, bibliography, catalog, etc.) or available from one primary source (the book, artist, publisher, Caldecott citation). When reviewing the media information listed in this section, please keep this key in mind.

- When hard data could not be found to confirm a book's media, the book's entry states, "Medium not known."

- Information from only one secondary source is included but marked by a question mark in parentheses after the medium/media.

We earnestly solicit corrections and additional information regarding Caldecott media. Our goal is to compile an accurate and complete list of the art media used to create all Caldecott Medal and Honor Books.

2014 AWARD

Locomotive by **Brian Floca, illustrated by the author.** ATHENEUM BOOKS FOR YOUNG READERS, AN IMPRINT OF SIMON & SCHUSTER CHILDREN'S PUBLISHING.

Watercolor, ink, acrylic, and gouache

Accompany a family on a weeklong train trip from Omaha to Sacramento in 1869. Brian Floca's dramatic illustrations incorporate meticulously-researched portraits of train, travelers, and crew as they traverse the American landscape on the new transcontinental railroad.

HONORS

Journey by **Aaron Becker, illustrated by the author,** CANDLEWICK.

Watercolor and pen & ink

Finding a magical red crayon, a bored, lonely girl draws a door on her bedroom wall that leads to a wondrous but perilous world. Drab, sepia-toned, humdrum reality gives way to sumptuous, lushly-hued landscapes.

Flora and the Flamingo by **Molly Idle, illustrated by the author.** CHRONICLE BOOKS LLC.

Prismacolor pencil on Canson, vellum finish Bristol

The budding relationship between an awkward young girl and a graceful flamingo is revealed through carefully orchestrated flaps. The minimalist setting, limited color palette, and use of white space and page turns create a timeless and joyful visual experience.

Mr. Wuffles! **by David Wiesner, illustrated by the author.** CLARION BOOKS, AN IMPRINT OF HOUGHTON MIFFLIN HARCOURT PUBLISHING COMPANY.

Watercolor and India ink

Mr. Wuffles finds a new toy that is actually a tiny spaceship in this nearly wordless science fiction tale of epic and miniature proportions. Crisp illustrations shine in an innovative graphic novel, picture book hybrid.

2013 AWARD

This Is Not My Hat **by Jon Klassen, illustrated by the author.** CANDLEWICK.

Chinese ink, digital

In this darkly humorous tale, a tiny fish knows it's wrong to steal a hat, but it fits him just right. Now the big fish wants his hat back. Klassen's controlled palette, opposing narratives, and subtle cues compel readers to follow the fish and imagine the consequence.

HONORS

Creepy Carrots! **by Aaron Reynolds, illustrated by Peter Brown.** SIMON & SCHUSTER BOOKS FOR YOUNG READERS, AN IMPRINT OF SIMON & SCHUSTER CHILDREN'S PUBLISHING DIVISION.

Pencil on paper, digitally composited and colored

Jasper the rabbit loves carrots until he is convinced they're coming for him! Pronounced shadows, black borders, and shaded edges enhance this ever so slightly sinister tale with a distinctly cinematic feel.

Extra Yarn **by Mac Barnett, illustrated by Jon Klassen.** BALZER + BRAY, AN IMPRINT OF HARPERCOLLINS PUBLISHERS.

Gouache, digital

A selfish archduke threatens to halt a girl's transformation of a colorless town and steal her magical yarn. Shifts of color signal character change and critical turns of plot—all done with just the right stitches of humor.

Green **by Laura Vaccaro Seeger, illustrated by the author.** NEAL PORTER BOOKS, AN IMPRINT OF ROARING BROOK PRESS.

Acrylic paint on canvas paper

Seeger engages all the senses with her fresh approach to the multiple meanings of "green." Using thickly-layered acrylics, word pairings, and cleverly placed die cuts, she invites readers to pause, pay attention, and wonder.

One Cool Friend, by Toni Buzzeo, illustrated by David Small. DIAL BOOKS FOR YOUNG READERS, A DIVISION OF PENGUIN YOUNG READERS GROUP.

Pen and ink, ink wash, watercolor, and colored pencil

Energetic line and dizzying perspective combine for a rollicking tale of Father, Elliot, and a highly improbable pet (or two). Buzzeo's text, brimming with sly wordplay, earns its perfect counterpoint in Small's illustrations with chilly details and visual jokes.

Sleep Like a Tiger by Mary Logue, illustrated by Pamela Zagarenski. HOUGHTON MIFFLIN BOOKS FOR CHILDREN, AN IMPRINT OF HOUGHTON MIFFLIN HARCOURT PUBLISHING COMPANY.

Mixed media paintings on wood, computer illustration

Surrounded with dreamlike images of crowns, ornate patterns, and repeated visual motifs, parents coax their little girl into bed for the night in this whimsical story with universal appeal.

2012 AWARD

A Ball for Daisy by Chris Raschka, illustrated by the author. SCHWARTZ & WADE BOOKS, AN IMPRINT OF RANDOM HOUSE CHILDREN'S BOOKS, A DIVISION OF RANDOM HOUSE, INC.

Ink, watercolor, and gouache

In a wordless book with huge children's appeal, Chris Raschka gives us the story of an irrepressible little dog whose most prized possession is accidently destroyed. With brilliant economy of line and color, Raschka captures Daisy's total (yet temporary) devastation. A buoyant tale of loss, recovery, and friendship.

HONORS

Blackout by John Rocco, illustrated by the author. DISNEY, HYPERION BOOKS, AN IMPRINT OF DISNEY BOOK GROUP.

Graphite pencil on Bristol paper and digital color

A summer's power outage draws an urban family up to their building's roof and then down to the street for an impromptu block party. Rocco illuminates details and characters with a playful use of light and shadow in his cartoon-style illustrations.

Grandpa Green by **Lane Smith, illustrated by the author.** ROARING BROOK PRESS, A DIVISION OF HOLTZBRINCK PUBLISHING HOLDINGS LIMITED PARTNERSHIP.

Characters rendered with brush and waterproof drawing ink
Foliage created with watercolor, oil paint, and digital paint

Elaborate topiary sculptures give visual form to memories in a wildly fanciful garden tended by a child and his beloved great-grandfather. Using an inspired palate, Smith invites readers to tour a green lifetime of meaningful moments.

Me . . . Jane by **Patrick McDonnell, illustrated by the author.** LITTLE, BROWN AND COMPANY, A DIVISION OF HACHETTE BOOK GROUP, INC.

India ink and watercolor on paper

Watching birds and squirrels in her yard, a young girl discovers the joy and wonder of nature. In delicate, precise strokes, McDonnell depicts the awakening of a scientific spirit. A perceptive glimpse of the childhood of primatologist Jane Goodall.

2011 AWARD

A Sick Day for Amos McGee by **Philip C. Stead, illustrated by Erin E. Stead.** A NEAL PORTER BOOK. ROARING BROOK PRESS, A DIVISION OF HOLTZBRINCK PUBLISHING.

Woodblock printing techniques and pencil

In this tender tale of reciprocity and friendship, zookeeper Amos McGee gets the sniffles and receives a surprise visit from his caring animal friends. Erin Stead's delicate woodblock prints and fine pencil work complement Philip Stead's understated, spare humorous text to create a well-paced, gentle, and satisfying book.

HONORS

Dave the Potter: Artist, Poet, Slave by **Laban Carrick Hill, illustrated by Bryan Collier.** LITTLE, BROWN AND COMPANY, A DIVISION OF HACHETTE BOOK GROUP, INC.

Watercolor/collage on 400-pound Arches watercolor paper

Collier's arrestingly beautiful artistic interpretation of Hill's poetic text reveals Dave the potter's artistic process while also conveying the dignified triumph of his humanity in the face of oppression. Lush, earth-toned, multimedia collages are illuminated in soft, ethereal light that focuses the eye on the subject of each spread.

Interrupting Chicken by David Ezra Stein, illustrated by the author. CANDLEWICK.

Watercolor, water-soluble crayon, china marker, pen, opaque white ink, and tea

Stein's hilarious story presents Little Chicken and her long-suffering Papa, who just wants to get through a bedtime story without his daughter's metafictive disruptions.

Exuberant artwork shifts media and style, taking readers into three fairy tales, culminating in Little Chicken's "Bedtime for Papa," but truly delivering a story for all.

2010 AWARD

The Lion & the Mouse by Jerry Pinkney, illustrated by the author. LITTLE, BROWN BOOKS FOR YOUNG READERS.

Pencil, watercolor, and colored pencils on paper

The screech of an owl, the squeak of a mouse, and the roar of a lion transport readers to the Serengeti plains for this virtually wordless retelling of Aesop's classic fable. In glowing colors, Pinkney's textured watercolor illustrations masterfully portray the relationship between two very unlikely friends.

HONORS

All the World by Liz Garton Scanlon, illustrated by Marla Frazee. BEACH LANE BOOKS, AN IMPRINT OF SIMON & SCHUSTER CHILDREN'S PUBLISHING.

Black Prismacolor pencil, watercolors on Strathmore 2-ply hotpress paper

Frazee's small vignettes and sweeping double-page spreads invite readers to share a joyful day with a diverse, multigenerational community. Flowing lines and harmonious colors give vibrant life to Scanlon's poetic text.

Red Sings from Treetops: A Year in Colors by Joyce Sidman, illustrated by Pamela Zagarenski. HOUGHTON MIFFLIN BOOKS FOR CHILDREN/HOUGHTON MIFFLIN HARCOURT.

Mixed media paintings on wood, computer illustration

Playful illustrations enliven Sidman's expressive poetry in this exploration of the seasons and their colors.

2009 AWARD

The House in the Night by Susan Marie Swanson, illustrated by Beth Krommes. HOUGHTON MIFFLIN.

Scratchboard and watercolor

Richly detailed black-and-white scratchboard illustrations expand this timeless bedtime verse, offering reassurance to young children that there is always light in the darkness.

HONORS

A Couple of Boys Have the Best Week Ever by Marla Frazee, illustrated by the author. HARCOURT.

Black Prismacolor and gouache on Stonehenge paper

In lively, detailed, subtly retro cartoons, Frazee gently pokes fun at adult expectations and captures the unbounded joy of two friends experiencing a parent-free summer adventure.

How I Learned Geography by Uri Shulevitz, illustrated by the author. FARRAR STRAUS GIROUX.

Collage, pen and ink, and watercolor

Recounting memories of his family's flight from the Warsaw blitz and his years as a refugee during World War II, Shulevitz employs watercolor and ink to depict a boy liberated from his dreary existence through flights of fancy.

A River of Words: The Story of William Carlos Williams by Jen Bryant, illustrated by Melissa Sweet. EERDMANS.

Watercolor, collage, and mixed media

Sweet's mixed-media collage and primitive watercolors flow seamlessly with Bryant's prose to reveal the important bits and pieces of Williams's ordinary yet extraordinary life as a doctor and poet.

2008 AWARD

The Invention of Hugo Cabret by Brian Selznick. SCHOLASTIC.

Pencil on Fabriano Artistico watercolor paper

Hugo is a young orphan secretly living in the walls of a train station where he labors to complete a mysterious invention left by his father. In a work of more than five hundred pages, the suspenseful text and wordless double-page spreads narrate the tale in turns. Black-and-white pencil illustrations evoke the flickering images of the silent films to which the book pays homage.

HONORS

Henry's Freedom Box: A True Story from the Underground Railroad by Ellen Levine, illustrated by Kadir Nelson. SCHOLASTIC.

Pencils, watercolor, and oil

Inspired by an antique lithograph, Nelson has created dramatically luminous illustrations that portray Henry "Box" Brown's ingenious design to ship himself in a box from slavery to freedom.

First the Egg **by Laura Vaccaro Seeger, illustrated by the author. ROARING BROOK PRESS/NEAL PORTER.**

Acrylic paint on canvas

This innovative concept book on transformations uses strategically placed die-cuts to provide an astonishing visual explication of the word "then." The richly textured brushstrokes creatively reveal the process of metamorphosis for young readers.

The Wall: Growing Up behind the Iron Curtain **by Peter Sís, illustrated by the author. FRANCES FOSTER/FARRAR STRAUS GIROUX.**

Fine marker plus red ink, pen and ink with wash, watercolors

In a graphic memoir of his youth in Prague, Sís brilliantly weds artistic and design choices to content: tight little panels with officious lines and red punctuation; full-bleed line-and-watercolor spreads of nightmares and dreams; color and absence of color.

Knuffle Bunny Too: A Case of Mistaken Identity **by Mo Willems, illustrated by the author. HYPERION.**

Hand-drawn ink sketches, colored and shaded digitally, and photography

Masterful photo collages take Trixie and her daddy through their now-familiar Brooklyn neighborhood to the pre-K class where Trixie discovers that her beloved Knuffle Bunny is not "so one-of-a-kind anymore."

2007 AWARD

Flotsam **by David Wiesner. CLARION.**

Watercolor

A vintage camera washed up on the beach provides a young boy with a surprising view of fantastical images from the bottom of the sea. From fish eye to lens eye, readers see a frame-by-frame narrative of lush marinescapes ebbing and flowing from the real to the surreal.

HONORS

Gone Wild: An Endangered Animal Alphabet **by David McLimans. WALKER.**

Pencil, pen, brush, india ink, bristol board, and computer

This black-and-white iconic alphabet is sophisticated enough to intrigue and captivate readers of any age. A contemporary interpretation of an illuminated alphabet melds animals and letters into twenty-six unique and elegant graphic images.

Moses: When Harriet Tubman Led Her People to Freedom by **Carole Boston Weatherford, illustrated by Kadir Nelson.** HYPERION/JUMP AT THE SUN.

Oil and watercolor paints applied over pencil drawings on paper

Nelson's dramatic renderings evoke the spiritual and physical journey of Harriet Tubman. Emotionally powerful images combined with poetically evocative text portray a strong woman who followed her star to an extraordinary destiny.

2006 AWARD

The Hello, Goodbye Window by **Norton Juster, illustrated by Chris Raschka.** MICHAEL DI CAPUA.

Watercolor, pastel crayons, charcoal pencil

In this sunny portrait of familial love, a little girl tells us about her everyday experiences visiting her grandparents' house. Raschka's style resembles the spontaneous drawings of children, perfectly mirroring the guileless young narrator's exuberant voice. White space balances the density of the layered colors, creating a visual experience that is surprisingly sophisticated.

HONORS

Rosa by **Nikki Giovanni, illustrated by Bryan Collier.** HENRY HOLT.

Watercolor, collage

From the arresting cover through the endpapers, *Rosa*, with Giovanni's spare, elegant prose and Collier's iconic illustrations, celebrates the quiet courage of Rosa Parks. Radiant watercolors of faces and hands highlighted against the edges of richly colored collages create a distinguished work of art.

Zen Shorts by **Jon J Muth, illustrated by the author.** SCHOLASTIC.

Watercolor and ink

Muth's story of inquisitive siblings befriending a wise panda is told through luminous watercolors interwoven with three lessons, set apart by starkly contrasting, Asian-inspired brush paintings. The interplay of artistic styles elegantly conveys the gentle, timeless messages of self-knowledge and acceptance.

Hot Air: The (Mostly) True Story of the First Hot-Air Balloon Ride by **Marjorie Priceman, illustrated by the author.** ANNE SCHWARTZ/ATHENEUM.

Gouache and india ink on watercolor paper

Energetic lines and rich watercolors animate this aerial adventure over eighteenth-century France. Priceman, who received a 1996 Caldecott honor for *Zin! Zin! Zin! A Violin*, combines spare text, dynamic design, and masterful perspective to illuminate the humor and high jinks of three animals swept up in the winds of history.

Song of the Water Boatman and Other Pond Poems by Joyce Sidman, illustrated by Beckie Prange. HOUGHTON MIFFLIN.

Woodblock hand-colored with watercolor

Eleven joyful songs of everyday pond life throughout the seasons are celebrated through this elegant and satisfying combination of visual drama, poetry, and scientific facts. The organic lines of Prange's exceptionally executed, hand-colored woodblock illustrations enlarge upon Sidman's expressive nature-themed poems.

2005 AWARD

Kitten's First Full Moon by Kevin Henkes, illustrated by the author. GREENWILLOW.

Gouache and colored pencil

Henkes employs boldly outlined organic shapes and shades of black, white, and gray with rose undertones on creamy paper to tell a simple story of a kitten who mistakes the moon for a bowl of milk. The moon, the flowers, the fireflies' lights, and the kitten's eyes create a comforting circle motif. The gouache and colored-pencil illustrations project a varied page design that rhythmically paces the spare text.

HONORS

The Red Book by Barbara Lehman, illustrated by the author. HOUGHTON MIFFLIN.

Watercolor, gouache, and ink

With a simplicity that belies their depth, Lehman's nuanced watercolor illustrations transport a city girl, an island boy, and the viewer beyond their familiar worlds. This wordless picture book offers an enticing visual journey with surprising twists and reveals the mysterious power of books.

Coming On Home Soon by Jacqueline Woodson, illustrated by E. B. Lewis. PUTNAM.

Watercolor on Arches paper

Evocative watercolor paintings illuminate a story of cross-generational love and convey the longing of a child anticipating her mother's return. Lewis's portraiture and attention to light sources, from cold winter hues to warm interior tones, reflect the loneliness of the child and the comforting strength of her grandmother.

Knuffle Bunny: A Cautionary Tale by Mo Willems, illustrated by the author. HYPERION.

Hand-drawn ink sketches and digital photography—combined using a computer, which was also used to color and shade the sketches and give the photographs a sepia tone

An ordinary trip to the laundromat with Dad becomes a hilarious epic drama of miscommunication when Trixie realizes that her beloved stuffed animal is left behind. This energetic comedy, illustrated with an unconventional combination of sepia-tone photographs and wry cartoon ink sketches, charms both parents and children.

2004 AWARD

The Man Who Walked between the Towers by Mordicai Gerstein, illustrated by the author. ROARING BOOK PRESS.

Pen and ink and oil paint on paper

This true story recounts the daring feat of a spirited young Frenchman who walked a tightrope between the World Trade Center twin towers in 1974. His joy in dancing on a thin wire high above Manhattan and the awe of the spectators in the streets far below are captured in exquisite ink and oil paintings that perfectly complement the spare, lyrical text.

HONORS

Ella Sarah Gets Dressed by Margaret Chodos-Irvine, illustrated by the author. HARCOURT.

Various printmaking techniques on Rives paper

Standing in front of her wardrobe, Ella Sarah selects her attire and makes her own fashion statement. Cheerful, bold colors outlined in white emphasize Ella Sarah's freedom and confidence. Pink polka-dots on an orange background and blue-green rickrack on the borders of the jacket flap foreshadow her unique outfit.

What Do You Do with a Tail like This? by Steve Jenkins and Robin Page, illustrated by the authors. HOUGHTON MIFFLIN.

Cut-paper collage

This innovative guessing book delivers a fun and playful science lesson on thirty animals' body parts: ears, eyes, mouths, noses, feet, and tails. The artist uses exquisite cut-paper collage to detail basic forms combined with clever placement of the spare text to create an interactive visual display.

Don't Let the Pigeon Drive the Bus! **by Mo Willems, illustrated by the author. HYPERION.**

Calligraphic cartoon drawings in dark marking pencil; scanned, cleaned, and colored in Photoshop

A persistent pigeon asks, pleads, cajoles, wheedles, connives, negotiates, demands, and uses emotional blackmail in attempts to get behind the wheel. Pigeon will not take no for an answer and puts the reader on the spot, using an escalating series of tactics. Perfectly paced, every line and blank space in the deceptively simple illustrations are essential to this distinguished work.

2003 AWARD

My Friend Rabbit **by Eric Rohmann, illustrated by the author. ROARING BROOK PRESS.**

Hand-colored relief prints (watercolors)

Mouse shares his brand-new toy airplane with his friend Rabbit, and no one can predict the disastrous—but hilarious—results. When the airplane lands in a tree, the chaos only builds as Rabbit drags, pushes, and carries the whole neighborhood, including Elephant, Hippo, and Crocodile, to aid in the rescue. Eric Rohmann's hand-colored relief prints express a vibrant energy through solid black outlines, lightly textured backgrounds, and a robust use of color.

HONORS

The Spider and the Fly **by Mary Howitt, illustrated by Tony DiTerlizzi. SIMON & SCHUSTER.**

Lamp black and titanium white holbein Acryla gouache and Berol Prismacolor pencil on Strathmore 5-ply, plate Bristol board and reproduced in silver and black duotone, graphite, and Adobe Photoshop

DiTerlizzi's wickedly delicious tribute to silent film—based on the cautionary tale penned by Mary Howitt in 1829—presents an old-fashioned cackling villain and a naive damsel in distress in this ambient, moody picture book with all the allure of the flickering silver screen. Skillful use of tone, line, and perspective add to the mystery of this melodramatic tale, executed entirely in eerie shades of black and white.

Hondo & Fabian **by Peter McCarty, illustrated by the author. HENRY HOLT.**

Pencil on watercolor paper

A beach outing for the dog and a full day at home for the cat are skillfully interwoven in this quiet tale of friendship. Spare text describes the day's events while soft, glowing illustrations tell the real story of parallel activities with subtle humor. McCarty's design choices from font and page layout to size and inviting cover art show great attention to detail in this masterfully executed picture book.

Noah's Ark by Jerry Pinkney, illustrated by the author. SeaStar.

Pencil, colored pencil, watercolors

In this striking rendition of Noah and the Great Flood, Jerry Pinkney has integrated the well-known story from Genesis with masterful pencil and watercolor illustrations to create a stunning whole. Vibrant paintings evoke the tone of the story from lush, sweeping views of the earth to intricate details of the massive ark, myriad animals, Noah and his family, and finally to the restoration of the planet.

2002 AWARD

The Three Pigs by David Wiesner, illustrated by the author. Clarion.

Watercolor, gouache, colored inks, pencil, and colored pencil on Fabriano hot press paper

In *The Three Pigs*, the plot and form of a familiar folktale unravel as the pigs are huffed and puffed off the page and into a new world. The trio cavorts through scenes from a nursery rhyme to a fairy tale, liberating other characters on the fly. Using a range of artistic styles and thrilling perspectives, Wiesner plays with the structure and conventions of traditional storytelling, redefining the picture book.

HONORS

Martin's Big Words: The Life of Dr. Martin Luther King, Jr. by Doreen Rappaport, illustrated by Bryan Collier. Jump at the Sun/Hyperion.

Watercolor, cut-paper collage

In this picture-book biography of Martin Luther King Jr., Rappaport's spare text and carefully chosen quotes are carried to a powerful emotional level by Collier's art. From the smiling, inviting image on the cover to each striking double spread the artist portrays significant events evoking King's purpose, telling readers that "his big words are alive for us today."

The Dinosaurs of Waterhouse Hawkins: An Illuminating History of Mr. Waterhouse Hawkins, Artist and Lecturer by Barbara Kerley, illustrated by Brian Selznick. Scholastic.

Acrylics

With a sense of showmanship echoing the spectacle of Waterhouse Hawkins's own public presentations, this dramatic biography brings the work of the nineteenth-century dinosaur artist to life. Using a rich palette, theatrical staging, and monumental dimensions, Selznick creates an exquisite balance between illustration and design in this distinguished marriage of science and art.

The Stray Dog: From a True Story by Reike Sassa **by Marc Simont, illustrated by the author.** HARPERCOLLINS.

Watercolor, gouache

A chance encounter turns into a family love affair in this disarmingly simple, gently humorous, and emotionally satisfying tale. The soft palette and subtle touches in the distinctive watercolors perfectly capture the heroic actions of the young protagonists and convey the universal feelings of longing and belonging.

2001 AWARD

So You Want to Be President? **by Judith St. George, illustrated by David Small.** PHILOMEL.

Watercolor, ink, and pastel chalk

In illustrations rendered in a harmonious mix of watercolor, ink, and pastel chalk, Small employs wiry and expansive lines that echo political cartooning and invest this personable history of the presidency with imaginative detail, wry humor, and refreshing dignity. Small's illustrations capture the spirit of each president featured and provide a genuinely enlightening overview of this unique American institution.

Published with revised text and art in 2004 (Philomel).

HONORS

Casey at the Bat: A Ballad of the Republic Sung in the Year 1888 **by Ernest L. Thayer, illustrated by Christopher Bing.** HANDPRINT.

Pen and ink scratchboard engravings

In the format of an 1888 scrapbook, the immortal ballad of Ernest Thayer finds new life in Christopher Bing's innovative treatment. Pen-and-ink scratchboard "engravings" in late nineteenth-century style seamlessly blend memorabilia and trompe l'oeil re-creations in an homage to the great American pastime.

Click, Clack, Moo: Cows That Type **by Doreen Cronin, illustrated by Betsy Lewin.** SIMON & SCHUSTER.

Watercolor

Farm-smart cows recycle a piece of outdated technology, a manual typewriter, to improve barnyard conditions. Lewin's illustrations help tell this tongue-in-cheek story about bovine agitators locking horns with Farmer Brown in a battle of will and wit that results in a comically satisfying conclusion.

Olivia **by Ian Falconer, illustrated by the author.** ANNE SCHWARTZ/ATHENEUM.

Charcoal and gouache

Olivia, an inquisitive, creative, confident young piglet, is "very good at wearing people out." With the touch of a minimalist, Falconer has created an exuberant character using deft black lines, delicate charcoal shading, generous white space, and spots of brilliant red.

2000 AWARD

Joseph Had a Little Overcoat **by Simms Taback, illustrated by the author.** VIKING.

Watercolor, gouache, pencil, ink, and collage

A resourceful and resilient tailor transforms his worn-out overcoat into smaller and smaller garments. The patchwork layout of the pages, the two-dimensional paintings, and the exaggerated perspectives, reminiscent of the folk art tradition, are the very fabric that turn this overcoat into a story.

HONORS

A Child's Calendar: Poems **by John Updike, illustrated by Trina Schart Hyman.** HOLIDAY HOUSE.

Pen and ink and watercolor

Twelve seasonal poems spanning the calendar year are accompanied by pen-and-ink and watercolor paintings that complement and enhance the text in this book of poetry. Hyman's affectionate illustrations expand Updike's poetic celebration of the changing of the seasons and holidays.

Sector 7 **by David Wiesner, illustrated by the author.** CLARION.

Watercolor

A small boy on a class trip to the Empire State Building is transported by a friendly cloud to Sector 7, a great cloud factory high in the sky. Wiesner's striking and dramatic watercolors transform the childhood fantasy of figures in the clouds into an imaginative story without words.

When Sophie Gets Angry—Really, Really Angry . . . **by Molly Bang, illustrated by the author.** BLUE SKY/SCHOLASTIC.

Gouache

Sophie's indignation over being required to share a favorite toy with her sister leads her on a lonely internal journey from anger to equilibrium. Bang's use of color, line, and visual onomatopoeia combine with a deceptively simple text to create a visually stunning color of a child's journey through a temper tantrum and back to the warmth of her family.

The Ugly Duckling, **adapted and illustrated by Jerry Pinkney.** MORROW.

Watercolor

Panoramic end papers set the scene for the creation of the familiar Hans Christian Andersen tale, *The Ugly Duckling.* Each full-page spread is lush with color that befits the beauty of the naturalistic setting. Pinkney imbues the animals with personality without anthropomorphizing them.

1999 AWARD

Snowflake Bentley by Jacqueline Briggs Martin, illustrated by Mary Azarian. HOUGHTON MIFFLIN.

Woodcuts, hand-tinted with watercolors

Mary Azarian's handsome woodcuts recall the impassioned life of a self-taught Vermont scientist, who as a boy was determined that one day his camera would capture the extraordinary and unique beauty of snowflakes.

HONORS

Duke Ellington: The Piano Prince and His Orchestra by Andrea Davis Pinkney, illustrated by Brian Pinkney. HYPERION.

Scratchboard renderings with gouache, luma dyes, and oil paint

Brian Pinkney masterfully uses color and movement to introduce today's children to the life and music of Duke Ellington, one of the great composers and jazz musicians of the twentieth century.

No, David! by David Shannon, illustrated by the author. BLUE SKY/SCHOLASTIC.

Acrylics and colored pencil

David, a typically mischievous preschooler, is into everything he shouldn't be and "No, David!" is his mother's constant refrain. Shannon's childlike paintings and inventive use of line, color, and perspective bring David to life.

Snow by Uri Shulevitz, illustrated by the author. FARRAR STRAUS GIROUX.

Ink and watercolor washes

This magical picture book captures in ink and watercolor washes the excitement of a small boy and his dog who, despite adult naysayers, steadfastly believe that snow is coming.

Tibet: Through the Red Box by Peter Sís, illustrated by the author. FRANCES FOSTER/FARRAR STRAUS GIROUX.

Watercolor, pen and ink, and oil pastel

Through detailed art and lyrical text, Sís takes the reader on a literal, spiritual, and symbolic journey through time and memory to his childhood, his separation from a father far away in Tibet, and finally their reunion.

1998 AWARD

Rapunzel by Paul O. Zelinsky, illustrated by the author. DUTTON.

Oil reproduced in full color

Zelinsky retells the story based on the familiar Grimm's folktale as well as earlier French and Italian sources. The detailed oil paintings are inspired by Renaissance Masters' paintings.

HONORS

The Gardener by Sarah Stewart, illustrated by David Small. FARRAR STRAUS GIROUX.

Watercolor, ink pen line, and crayon

Illustrations, combined with letters home, tell the story of Lydia Grace Finch, a young Depression-era heroine, who transforms her curmudgeonly uncle and his dreary urban neighborhood with her rooftop garden.

Harlem: A Poem by Walter Dean Myers, illustrated by Christopher Myers. SCHOLASTIC.

Ink, gouache, and cut-paper collage

Christopher Myers uses ink, gouache, and cut-paper collage to interpret his father's ode to Harlem. A kaleidoscope of words and images leads the reader on a musical journey filled with sass and swing.

There Was an Old Lady Who Swallowed a Fly by Simms Taback, illustrated by the author. VIKING.

Mixed media and collage on kraft paper in color

The popular American folk song of the old woman with an insatiable taste for life is served up in a fresh presentation. The reader is treated to an insider's view of her progressively excessive appetite through expanding die-cut peepholes to the inevitable climax.

1997 AWARD

Golem by David Wisniewski, illustrated by the author. CLARION.

Color-aid, coral, and bark cut papers

The Jews in sixteenth-century Prague turn to their rabbi during time of trouble. The Golem, created to protect the Jews, reflects the themes of power and redemption. How the rabbi deals with the soulless clay giant is a tale that is detailed through intricate paper-cuts.

HONORS

Hush! A Thai Lullaby by **Minfong Ho, illustrated by Holly Meade. ORCHARD.**

Cut-paper collage with ink

A strong visual narrative tells the story of a mother who warns a crying mosquito, a leaping frog, and a swinging monkey not to waken her sleeping child. This is a gentle, cumulative bedtime story, sure to please and settle down children.

The Graphic Alphabet by **David Pelletier, illustrated by the author. ORCHARD.**

Computer-generated images reproduced in full color

This alphabet book uses computer imagery laced with wit and humor to help young children learn the letters. Each letter is not only represented by a word, image, or concept but also is the word, image, or concept. Crisp imagery is combined with meticulous design.

The Paperboy by **Dav Pilkey, illustrated by the author. ORCHARD.**

Acrylics and india ink

A boy wakes in the darkness, bundles his newspapers, and accompanied by his faithful dog delivers the daily papers to the still, dark houses. Carefully balanced compositions and a restrained but rich palette give this story tremendous visual appeal.

Starry Messenger: A Book Depicting the Life of a Famous Scientist, Mathematician, Astronomer, Philosopher, Physicist, Galileo Galilei by **Peter Sís, illustrated by the author. FRANCES FOSTER/FARRAR STRAUS GIROUX.**

Pen and brown ink and watercolor

Galileo Galilei's story is illustrated in a style that evokes Renaissance art, architecture, and cartography. The events of his everyday life, the struggles and successes, are captured through detailed attention on each page, which brings to life the world on the verge of discovery.

1996 AWARD

Officer Buckle and Gloria by **Peggy Rathmann, illustrated by the author. PUTNAM.**

Watercolor and ink

Police dog Gloria's irreverent acrobatics behind Safety Officer Buckle's back contrast with the officer's straight-laced safety tips to school audiences. Original, lively, and energetic art leads the readers through a story of cooperation and friendship. Watercolor and ink illustrations employ brilliant colors that, combined with a creative use of white space, engage the reader in the humor and warmth of this stellar performance.

HONORS

Alphabet City by Stephen T. Johnson, illustrated by the author. VIKING.

Pastels, watercolors, gouache, and charcoal on hot pressed watercolor paper

Photorealistic paintings of urban environment present an imaginative variety of views and perspectives, textures, and light. Each painting stands alone as a handsome, balanced piece. Together they are an inspiring exercise in seeing patterns and art in everyday things.

Zin! Zin! Zin! a Violin by Lloyd Moss, illustrated by Marjorie Priceman. SIMON & SCHUSTER.

Gouache

This exuberant introduction to the orchestra is a true celebration of music. The sense of visual musicality is enhanced by warm, changing background colors. The musicians themselves are far from static, and the text has rhythm and punch, changing size and moving across the pages in swoops and swirls to reflect the flow of music.

The Faithful Friend by Robert D. San Souci, illustrated by Brian Pinkney. SIMON & SCHUSTER.

Scratchboard and oil

Pinkney's distinctive illustrations evoke the mystery, magic, and romance in San Souci's retelling of this West Indian folktale. The unique scratchboard style, enhanced by vivid oil colors, is a superb match for this atmospheric story in which the main characters confront and ultimately overcome the dark forces of evil.

Tops & Bottoms, adapted and illustrated by Janet Stevens. HARCOURT BRACE.

Watercolor, colored pencil, and gesso on paper made by hand by Ray Tomasso, Denver, Colorado

Sleepy, sprawling bear is outwitted by the wily hare, who succeeds in feeding his numerous offspring with abundant vegetable harvests. Handmade vegetable paper and a masterful use of mixed media contribute to this zesty, organic combination of story and illustration.

1995 AWARD

Smoky Night by Eve Bunting, illustrated by David Diaz. HARCOURT BRACE.

Acrylic paintings set against mixed media collage backgrounds

Inspired by the Los Angeles riots, *Smoky Night* relates the happenings of a night of urban rioting from a child's perspective. With thickly textured, expressionistic acrylic paintings set against mixed-media collages, Diaz creates dramatic, groundbreaking illustrations of the night's events. Both language and illustration convey the universal importance of human interaction through the personal story of one little boy and his cat.

HONORS

Swamp Angel by Anne Isaacs, illustrated by Paul O. Zelinsky. DUTTON.

Oil on cherry, maple, and birch veneers

In this original tall tale, Angelica Longrider, known as Swamp Angel, wrestles the huge bear Thundering Tarnation to save the winter supplies of settlers in Tennessee. With his whimsical illustrations, Paul O. Zelinsky has created a memorable heroine with the grit and gusto of a Paul Bunyan. Primitive-style oil paintings on cherry, maple, and birch veneers capture the folksy feel of life in nineteenth-century Tennessee.

John Henry by Julius Lester, illustrated by Jerry Pinkney. DIAL.

Pencil, colored pencil, and watercolor

Pinkney's earthy, craggy pencil and watercolor illustrations capture both the power and the humanity of this African-American folk-hero. Masterful use of light and shadow portray the strength and mass of the Allegheny Mountains, which match the magnitude of John Henry, while delicate shading and mottled color suggest the detail of a realistic natural setting enlivened with touches of whimsy.

Time Flies by Eric Rohmann, illustrated by the author. CROWN.

Oil

Stunning oil paintings in this wordless picture book dramatically portray a bird's flight though a museum display into the age of the living dinosaurs, where it encounters creatures vastly larger than itself. Rohmann uses rich, realistic shading; texture; and varying perspectives to create the bird's fanciful journey back to the time of its primitive ancestors.

1994 AWARD

Grandfather's Journey by Allen Say, illustrated by the author.
HOUGHTON MIFFLIN.

Watercolor

Grandfather's Journey eloquently portrays a Japanese immigrant's travels to a new land. Exquisite watercolors portray vast landscapes along with intimate family portraits that communicate hope, dignity, sadness, and love. Say powerfully connects the personal and the universal to create a rare harmony of longing and belonging.

HONORS

Peppe the Lamplighter by Elisa Bartone, illustrated by Ted Lewin. LOTHROP.

Watercolor

Lewin vividly captures the bustling market scenes, bleak tenement rooms, and the lamplit streets of turn-of-the-century New York's Little Italy. Dramatic watercolors portray young Peppe's struggle to help support his immigrant family and to win his father's respect.

In the Small, Small Pond **by Denise Fleming, illustrated by the author. HENRY HOLT.**

Colored cotton pulp poured through hand-cut stencils

Bright colors and lively language describe the cycle of pond life. Rhyming alliterative text and vibrant illustrations are filled with movement and fun in a joyous celebration of the natural world.

Owen **by Kevin Henkes, illustrated by the author. GREENWILLOW.**

Watercolor paints and black ink

A preschooler mouse, Owen, and his concerned parents confront a classic childhood drama: releasing the trusty, fuzzy blanket. Confident economical line and inspired layout convey Owen's spirited tenacity as he dances toward greater independence.

Raven: A Trickster Tale from the Pacific Northwest **by Gerald McDermott, illustrated by the author. HARCOURT BRACE JOVANOVICH.**

Gouache, colored pencil, and pastel on heavyweight, cold-press watercolor paper

McDermott reshapes the familiar trickster tale from the Pacific Northwest in which Raven steals light from the Sky Chief and brings it to people. Raven's spirit world is boldly colored and hard-edged, a strong graphic contrast to the soft watercolor background of the real Northwest landscape.

Yo! Yes? **by Chris Raschka, illustrated by the author. ORCHARD.**

Watercolor and charcoal pencil

Through bold, original use of line and angle, color and space, Raschka celebrates friendship and offers a timeless message about taking risks. The brief, rhythmic text invites enthusiastic sharing.

1993 AWARD

Mirette on the High Wire **by Emily Arnold McCully, illustrated by the author. PUTNAM.**

Watercolor

Emily Arnold McCully's vivid impressionistic watercolors bring nineteenth-century Paris to life with the story of Mirette, a spirited, risk-taking little girl. Mirette enables the former high-wire star Bellini to conquer his fear while achieving her own dream. Light, color, line, and movement in these animated and bold illustrations are in perfect balance with the text.

HONORS

The Stinky Cheese Man & Other Fairly Stupid Tales by Jon Scieszka, illustrated by Lane Smith. VIKING.

Oil and mixed media

The Little Red Hen talks in red letters and the giant talks in capitals in this irreverent retelling of the gingerbread man and other time-honored tales. The avant-garde art ("rendered in oil and vinegar" according to the book note) lampoons twentieth-century art in the process. Interdependence of words, visual images, and even the process of book design and publication extract every possible laugh in this outrageous collaboration.

Working Cotton by Sherley Anne Williams, illustrated by Carole Byard. HARCOURT BRACE JOVANOVICH.

Acrylic on Stonehenge white paper

Carole Byard's dramatic paintings portray the dignity of hard work and the strength of family relationships that are part of this migrant family's life. From the first glimpses of a streaky dawn to the red twilight, powerful, glowing portraits and landscapes poignantly complement the child's poetic depiction of the long workday.

Seven Blind Mice by Ed Young, illustrated by the author. PHILOMEL.

Paper collage

In this successful reinterpretation of the Indian fable of the blind man and the elephant, deceptively simple text integrates concepts of color, numbers, and days of the week with visual irony. Contrasting textured paper heightens the bold color and strong composition, while white typeface against a glossy background and marbleized endpapers add to the excellent design.

1992 AWARD

Tuesday by David Wiesner, illustrated by the author. CLARION.

Watercolor

Flying frogs on lily pads create mischief as they move from the fen to a small town on a Tuesday evening. The story ends with a comic twist suggesting more fantastic flights for the following Tuesday. Wiesner's watercolor illustrations show masterful use of light and dark, alternating perspectives, and variation in page design in this nine-word book.

HONOR

Tar Beach **by Faith Ringgold, illustrated by the author. CROWN.**

Acrylic on canvas

Child Cassie flies high above New York City in the 1930s, high above the quilt squares that ground each page, high above the busyness and conflict of everyday life, from family rooftop picnics to daddy's construction work. Acrylic paintings on canvas paper form the basis of this visual feast celebrating the act of transformation, while the quilt form represents a historically important African-American communication medium.

1991 AWARD

Black and White **by David Macaulay, illustrated by the author. HOUGHTON MIFFLIN.**

"Seeing Things"—watercolor; "Problem Parents"—ink line and wash; "A Waiting Game"—watercolor and gouache; "Udder Confusion"—gouache paint

Macaulay interweaves fantasy and reality in a tale of parents, trains, and cows. The author recommends careful inspection of words and pictures to both minimize and enhance confusion.

HONORS

Puss in Boots **by Charles Perrault, translated by Malcolm Arthur, illustrated by Fred Marcellino. MICHAEL DI CAPUA/FARRAR STRAUS GIROUX.**

Colored pencil on taupe-textured illustration paper

Large pale type and golden-toned paintings work brilliantly together providing an elegant regal look to the familiar fairy tale of Puss. With varied perspectives and points of view, Marcellino re-creates the French court and countryside to ingenious, often droll, effect.

"More, More, More," Said the Baby: 3 Love Stories **by Vera B. Williams. GREENWILLOW.**

Gouache paints; lettering painted in watercolor based on Gill Sans Extra Bold Print

Brightly framed gouache paintings reflect each child's sense of security and joy as a loving adult "catches" that baby up. This creative use of color, shape, and rhythm marks a unique and distinctive celebration of family life.

1990 AWARD

Lon Po Po: A Red-Riding Hood Story from China by Ed Young, translated and illustrated by the author. PHILOMEL.

Watercolor and pastels

Suspense and drama are lightened with bits of humor as the wolf Lon Po Po tries to trick three children into letting him into their house. Though he succeeds, the children quickly turn the tables on the wily animal. The artist uses vivid watercolors and pastels to create dramatic panel pictures.

HONORS

Color Zoo by Lois Ehlert, illustrated by the author. LIPPINCOTT.

Paper collage and die-cut forms

Vibrant colors and overlays of geometric-shaped cutouts in heavy paper combine to create expressive animal faces. The text is simply a one-word identification of the shape or animal. All of the action is in the creative paper engineering.

Hershel and the Hanukkah Goblins by Eric Kimmel, illustrated by Trina Schart Hyman. HOLIDAY HOUSE.

India ink and acrylic paint

Eight goblins haunt the old synagogue, preventing the villagers from celebrating Hanukkah until Hershel arrives to outwit all of the creatures. The dark illustrations are charged with energy as they show the imaginatively wicked goblins trying to frighten Hershel away.

Bill Peet: An Autobiography by Bill Peet, illustrated by the author. HOUGHTON MIFFLIN.

Pencil

From the time he learned to manipulate a crayon, drawing has been a consuming passion for Bill Peet. He tells how that passion affected his life, from childhood, through his work at the Disney Studios, to his life as an author. Using his usual artistic style, Peet has filled his autobiography with new black-and-white illustrations.

The Talking Eggs: A Folktale from the American South by Robert D. San Souci, illustrated by Jerry Pinkney. DIAL.

Pencil, colored-pencil, and watercolor

Running away from her angry mother and spoiled sister, Blanche is befriended by a strange old woman who owns a cow with two heads and chickens that lay talking eggs. The eerie and suspenseful black folktale is filled with watercolor pictures of deep woods and strange sights.

1989 AWARD

Song and Dance Man **by Karen Ackerman, illustrated by Stephen Gammell. KNOPF.**

Line drawings in colored pencil

When his grandchildren come to visit, Grandpa whisks them up to the attic, where he performs an exciting vaudeville routine. The colored-pencil sketches are alive with movement and drama.

HONORS

Mirandy and Brother Wind **by Patricia C. McKissack, illustrated by Jerry Pinkney. KNOPF.**

Pencil and watercolor

A sparkling, energetic Mirandy vows to dance with the wind at her first cakewalk— but to do that, she must catch it first. Lush, expansive illustrations of the rural South capture the vigor and imagination of the story.

Goldilocks and the Three Bears, **retold and illustrated by James Marshall. DIAL.**

Pen and ink and watercolor

The antithesis of the typical sweet, demure Goldilocks, this little girl with her bouncing golden ringlets is brash, irreverent, and captivating. Set in the present day, the briefly told nursery story abounds with color, humor, and wit.

The Boy of the Three-Year Nap **by Diane Snyder, illustrated by Allen Say. HOUGHTON MIFFLIN.**

Brush-line, pen and ink, and watercolor

Taro has earned his nickname because of his laziness and penchant for sleeping. When he turns trickster to stop his industrious mother's nagging, she in turn outwits him. The handsome pictures are noticeably influenced by eighteenth-century Japanese woodcuts and reflect the culture of the land where this folktale originated.

Free Fall, **illustrated by David Wiesner. LOTHROP.**

Watercolor

In a book made more powerful because it has no words to stifle the imagination, a boy falls asleep and dreams of fantastic adventures. In this visual story, the objects around the boy evolve from one thing into another and then back to their original shapes.

1988 AWARD

Owl Moon **by Jane Yolen, illustrated by John Schoenherr. PHILOMEL.**

Pen and ink and watercolor

Late one quiet winter's night, a little girl and her father go owling, watching and listening for the signs that say a great horned owl is nearby. Blue-toned color washes and simple landscapes create a frosty, magical night perfect for owl watching.

HONOR

Mufaro's Beautiful Daughters: An African Tale **by John Steptoe, illustrated by the author. LOTHROP.**

Crosshatched pen and ink and watercolor

Of the two sisters, one kind and good, the other mean and deceitful, only one will be chosen to marry the king. Dramatic yet realistic paintings in lush, jewel-toned colors illustrate this folktale from Zimbabwe.

1987 AWARD

Hey, Al **by Arthur Yorinks, illustrated by Richard Egielski. FARRAR STRAUS GIROUX.**

Watercolor

Janitor Al and his dog are swept away from their apparently humdrum lives by a huge bird that takes them to what at first seems like paradise. Full-color illustrations provide florid scenes of that paradise.

HONORS

The Village of Round and Square Houses **by Ann Grifalconi, illustrated by the author. LITTLE, BROWN.**

Pastels (?)

Pastel drawings are used to illustrate the story of the remote Cameron village of Tos where the women live in the round houses and the men live in the square ones so that each has a place to be together and a place to be apart.

Alphabatics **by Suse MacDonald, illustrated by the author. BRADBURY.**

Cells, vinyl acrylic; gouache

Brightly colored letters of the alphabet become acrobats as they twist and turn until they become the objects that represent the letters: A becomes an ark, J becomes a jack-in-the-box, S becomes a swan.

Rumpelstiltskin: From the German of the Brothers Grimm, **retold and illustrated by Paul O. Zelinsky.** DUTTON.

Oil paintings

When the proud father tells the king that his daughter can spin straw into gold, it is the tiny Rumpelstiltskin who actually does the spinning—for the price of the first-born child. Golden-toned, full-color oil paintings in medieval style retell this tale based on an early Brothers Grimm version.

1986 AWARD

The Polar Express **by Chris Van Allsburg, illustrated by the author.** HOUGHTON MIFFLIN.

Full-color oil pastel on pastel paper

Dark, brooding illustrations with unusual perspectives set the mood for a magical and poignant train ride. It is Christmas Eve when the young boy boards the train for a trip to the North Pole. There he receives a special gift from Santa Claus.

HONORS

The Relatives Came **by Cynthia Rylant, illustrated by Stephen Gammell.** BRADBURY.

Graphite and colored pencil

What a marvelous time is had when all the relatives come from Virginia for a visit! They crowd into the house, where there is much loving and hugging and breathing to do together! The pictures nearly bounce off the pages with all the love and happiness in this book.

King Bidgood's in the Bathtub **by Audrey Wood, illustrated by Don Wood.** HARCOURT BRACE JOVANOVICH.

Oil on pressed wood (?)

When the court is in a dither because the king refuses to get out of the bathtub, only the young page knows what to do. Illustrations reminiscent of an opera stage setting show off the full glory of the court scenes.

1985 AWARD

Saint George and the Dragon: A Golden Legend, **adapted from Edmund Spenser's** *Faerie Queen* **by Margaret Hodges, illustrated by Trina Schart Hyman. LITTLE, BROWN.**

India ink and acrylic

Lady Una and George, a knight of the Red Cross, must find and battle the terrible dragon that ruins the land. Hyman's illustrations tell the story dramatically, and the reader seems to look at the scenes through an iron-encased window.

HONORS

Hansel and Gretel, **retold by Rika Lesser, illustrated by Paul O. Zelinsky. DODD, MEAD.**

Oil paintings

In this book translated from one of the less-embellished versions of the classic Brothers Grimm story, the artwork dominates. Sometimes imitating sixteenth- and seventeenth-century Flemish art, sometimes adopting a romantic nineteenth-century style, the paintings are rich in color and detail.

The Story of Jumping Mouse, **retold and illustrated by John Steptoe. LOTHROP.**

Graphite pencil and india ink on paper

Large, expressive pencil drawings help tell the tale of a field mouse's search for the Far-Off Land. Armed with courage and hope, the mouse overcomes many obstacles until it is transformed into an eagle. The text is freely adapted from an unidentified Native American "why" story.

Have You Seen My Duckling? **by Nancy Tafuri, illustrated by the author. GREENWILLOW.**

Watercolors and pastels

In this almost wordless book, a duck asks the creatures of the pond if they have seen her lost duckling. Bright, clear illustrations show the adventuresome duckling, who is always seen a little hidden from but close to his mother.

1984 AWARD

The Glorious Flight: Across the Channel with Louis Blériot, July 25, 1909 **by Alice and Martin Provensen, illustrated by the authors. VIKING.**

Acrylic and pen and ink

Once he sees a flying machine, Louis Blériot becomes passionately interested in building his own machine and is successful on his eleventh attempt. Based on a true incident in France in the early 1900s, the biography is illustrated with pictures of shifting perspectives and touches of humor and views of a family growing older.

HONORS

Ten, Nine, Eight by Molly Bang, illustrated by the author. GREENWILLOW.

Gouache (poster paint)

Bedtime becomes a favorite time as the countdown begins. In a lulling rhyme, all of the things in a little girl's room are counted. The quiet time shared between father and daughter is illustrated with warm colors.

Little Red Riding Hood, retold and illustrated by Trina Schart Hyman. HOLIDAY HOUSE.

Ink and acrylic (?)

The familiar story of the little girl who goes to visit her grandmother subtly warns children not to talk to strangers. The detailed illustrations seem to place the setting of the story in New England.

1983 AWARD

Shadow by Blaise Cendrars, translated and illustrated by Marcia Brown. SCRIBNER.

Collage: paper, woodcuts, acrylics

Translated from the French poet Blaise Cendrars's work, this symbolic mood piece reflects stories told by African storytellers and shamans around a nighttime fire. Rich colors with black cutout accents create the visual image of the prowling, dancing, mute shadow.

HONORS

When I Was Young in the Mountains by Cynthia Rylant, illustrated by Diane Goode. DUTTON.

Watercolor and fine-colored pencil

The author affectionately recalls a childhood spent with her family in the Appalachian Mountains of West Virginia. Warm family scenes are filled with friendly, happy people. Many of the illustrations drift off into the mountain mist and bring a peacefulness to the recalled pleasures.

A Chair for My Mother by Vera B. Williams, illustrated by the author. GREENWILLOW.

Watercolor

After a fire destroys their home, a little girl, her waitress mother, and the girl's grandmother move into an apartment. They start saving all their coins for a big, comfortable chair for Mama and Grandma. The watercolor paintings have a suitably childlike look.

1982 AWARD

Jumanji by Chris Van Allsburg, illustrated by the author. HOUGHTON MIFFLIN.

Conté pencil with conté dust

Looking for something to do on a boring afternoon, Peter and Judy decide to try the strange board game they find in the park. Boredom vanishes as every space on which they land comes to life. Meticulously crafted black-and-white illustrations bring the game alive.

HONORS

Where the Buffaloes Begin by Olaf Baker, illustrated by
Stephen Gammell. WARNE.

Pencil drawings (?)

Majestic, haunting, and moody gray-toned illustrations show Little Wolf on his journey to the sacred place where buffaloes are said to originate. The rich prose was first published in *St. Nicholas Magazine* in 1915.

On Market Street by Arnold Lobel, illustrated by Anita Lobel. GREENWILLOW.

Watercolor and pen and ink

A nursery rhyme-like verse breaks into a celebration of all the wares—from A to Z—that a little boy purchases on Market Street. The illustrations, based on seventeenth-century French trade engravings, show brightly colored shopkeepers composed of their merchandise.

Outside over There by Maurice Sendak, illustrated by the author. HARPER & ROW.

Medium not known

When Ida is not focusing her complete attention on her baby sister, the baby is kidnapped by hooded goblins and replaced by a baby made of ice. Elaborate paintings combine romantic and surrealistic effects and are filled with subtleties and symbolism.

A Visit to William Blake's Inn: Poems for Innocent and Experienced Travelers
by Nancy Willard, illustrated by Alice and Martin Provensen.
HARCOURT BRACE JOVANOVICH.

Medium not known

Lyrical poems written in the spirit of William Blake combine with captivatingly imaginative illustrations that reflect the staidness and the whimsy of the eighteenth century. Nancy Willard also won the 1982 Newbery Award for this book.

1981 AWARD

Fables **by Arnold Lobel, illustrated by the author. HARPER & ROW.**

Gouache and pencil

Twenty original, brief, and witty animal fables, each complete with a moral, expose human foibles. Each fable is faced with a full-page painting in soft, rich colors that show the droll animals at the crucial moment of the fable.

HONORS

The Grey Lady and the Strawberry Snatcher **by Molly Bang, illustrated by the author. FOUR WINDS.**

Watercolor, sometimes with white gouache undercoat on gray construction paper

An old lady who, except for her hands and face, appears as a grey silhouette, buys a basket of strawberries and proceeds home, pursued by a strawberry snatcher. Interesting colors and textures are effectively combined with negative grey shapes in this vivid visual hide-and-seek game.

Truck **by Donald Crews, illustrated by the author. GREENWILLOW.**

Four halftone separations with black line drawings

Bright colors and geometric shapes roll across the pages as a truck carries a cargo of tricycles to its destination. There is no text. From the loading dock, through intricate highway systems, past road signs, to a truck stop, in clear and stormy weather, the big red truck moves its precious cargo across the country.

Mice Twice **by Joseph Low, illustrated by the author. MARGARET K. McELDERRY/ ATHENEUM.**

Watercolor and pen and ink (?)

Cat is very hungry and wants a nice tender mouse to eat, so he invites Mouse to dinner. Things escalate until even Lion and Crocodile are involved. It is Wasp who settles things in this funny tale that is enhanced through whimsical drawings.

The Bremen-Town Musicians, **retold and illustrated by Ilse Plume. DOUBLEDAY.**

Colored pencil and graphite (?)

Four animals, all unwanted, set out together to become musicians but instead end up outwitting a band of robbers. The Brothers Grimm tale is illustrated with glowing, subdued colors and rounded shapes.

1980 AWARD

Ox-Cart Man by Donald Hall, illustrated by Barbara Cooney. VIKING.

Acrylics on gesso-coated board

Clean, uncluttered paintings capture the flavor of nineteenth-century New England as a family's day-to-day life is mandated by the changing season. There is a strong sense of the passage of time and rhythm of life in this book.

HONORS

Ben's Trumpet by Rachel Isadora, illustrated by the author. GREENWILLOW/MORROW.

Pen and ink

The mood, sounds, and rhythms of jazz pulsate through the illustrations as Ben sits on the fire escape and blows his imaginary trumpet to the jazz sounds emanating from the Zig Zig Jazz Club. Set in the twenties and illustrated with dynamic black-and-white drawings, this is the story of one boy's dream coming true.

The Treasure by Uri Shulevitz, illustrated by the author. FARRAR STRAUS GIROUX.

Watercolor with black line on acetate

A poor man dreams that he must go to the castle bridge and wait for something that will turn about his fortunes. Traveling far to get there, he learns that the treasure is under his own stove. Illustrations with softly glowing colors and a striking use of light depict traditional eastern European villages and countrysides.

The Garden of Abdul Gasazi by Chris Van Allsburg, illustrated by the author. HOUGHTON MIFFLIN.

Carbon pencil on Strathmore paper

Illusion and reality become blurred when the unruly dog the boy has been tending runs away into the secret, foreboding garden of a retired magician. The visual perspectives and the play of light on the gray pencil drawings create an eerie, mysterious feeling.

1979 AWARD

The Girl Who Loved Wild Horses by Paul Goble, illustrated by the author. BRADBURY.

Full-color pen and ink and watercolor

The kinship is so strong between a Plains Indian girl and the horses she has lived with since becoming lost in a storm, that eventually she becomes one of them. Sharp, brilliantly colored paintings sweep across the pages and are in perfect harmony with the story.

HONORS

Freight Train **by Donald Crews, illustrated by the author.**
GREENWILLOW/MORROW.

Preseparated art; airbrush with transparent dyes

Large pictures of the different freight cars are identified by name and by color. Soon the train begins to move into a blur of colors as it swiftly goes on its way.

The Way to Start a Day **by Byrd Baylor, illustrated by Peter Parnall. SCRIBNER.**

Pen and ink (?)

A vibrant sunflower yellow and other colors blend with crisp, black lines to make effective use of symbolism in celebration of the sun. Poetic prose tells how cultures throughout the ages have sung to the new day's sun to honor it.

1978 AWARD

Noah's Ark **by Peter Spier, illustrated by the author. DOUBLEDAY.**

F pencil on paper; watercolor and white pencil; negatives scratched

The only text is the seventeenth-century Dutch poem, "The Flood," by Jacobus Revius, that opens the book. The rest of the book is a visual interpretation of Noah and his unbelievably difficult task of tending the animals on the ark. Careful details and softly hued watercolors depict the story with reverence, humor, and delight.

HONORS

Castle **by David Macaulay, illustrated by the author. HOUGHTON MIFFLIN.**

Pen and ink

Macaulay traces in text and drawings the step-by-step construction of a fictitious thirteenth-century English castle in Wales from its conception to its baptism by fire—a direct attack by hundreds of Welsh soldiers. The complex engineering task is generously illustrated with detailed black-and-white line drawings and diagrams.

It Could Always Be Worse: A Yiddish Folktale, **retold and illustrated by**
Margot Zemach. FARRAR STRAUS GIROUX.

Watercolor (?)

Crowded into one room with his mother, wife, and six children, a man goes to the rabbi for help. The rabbi's answer is to bring one animal after another to live in the house. Dynamic, earth-toned paintings with an eastern European look capture the humor of the rabbi's good advice.

1977 AWARD

Ashanti to Zulu: African Traditions by Margaret Musgrove, illustrated by Leo and Diane Dillon. DIAL.

Pastels, watercolors, and acrylics

Twenty-six different African tribal traditions and customs are introduced using the English alphabet as the vehicle. A border on each page frames the text and illustrations, where glowing colors mix with rich browns. The attention to authentic detail in each painting is remarkable.

HONORS

Hawk, I'm Your Brother by Byrd Baylor, illustrated by Peter Parnall. SCRIBNER.

Pen and ink (?)

In a gentle story told in simple, poetic prose, a young Native American boy wants desperately to fly like a hawk. Spacious, clean, panoramic line drawings convey the yearning of the boy and the power of the hawk.

Fish for Supper by M. B. Goffstein, illustrated by the author. DIAL.

Ink drawings

This quiet story chronicles the simple daily routine of Grandma, whose life centers around fishing. The black-and-white line drawings are centered in a square border of white space.

The Contest, retold and illustrated by Nonny Hogrogian. GREENWILLOW/MORROW.

Colored pencils and crayons for full color; pencil drawings for black and white

Realizing that they are both engaged to the same woman and each unwilling to give her up, two robbers compare their cleverness in thievery to see who deserves her. Large, colorful illustrations capture the flavor of the Armenian culture in this humorous folktale.

The Golem by Beverly Brodsky McDermott, illustrated by the author. LIPPINCOTT.

Gouache, watercolor, dye, and ink

The somber Jewish legend of the Golem, a creature created from clay that becomes more powerful and terrible than the evil he was made to destroy, is re-created with high visual drama. Striking paintings, vibrant with deep, rich colors, are filled with symbolism and massive shapes.

The Amazing Bone by William Steig, illustrated by the author.
FARRAR STRAUS GIROUX.

Watercolor (?)

On her way home from school, hapless heroine Pearl Pig finds an amazing talking bone. When the delectable piglet is waylaid by a debonair fox, the amazing bone saves Pearl. Sunny, fresh, springtime landscapes provide the background for the well-dressed characters.

1976 AWARD

Why Mosquitoes Buzz in People's Ears: A West African Tale, retold by Verna Aardema, illustrated by Leo and Diane Dillon. DIAL.

India ink; watercolor; pastels; vellum and frisket masks

Mosquito tells Iguana a tall tale about yams that annoys Iguana so much that he puts sticks in his ears so he cannot hear such things. Thus begins a chain reaction tale of the West African jungle. Illustrations show highly stylized animals.

HONORS

The Desert Is Theirs by Byrd Baylor, illustrated by Peter Parnall. SCRIBNER.

Pen and ink (?)

A spare, lyrical text tells of the relationship of the Papagos people to their environment—"we share . . . we only share." The paintings are dramatic and are reminiscent of the layers of colors found in sand paintings.

Strega Nona: An Old Tale by Tomie dePaola, illustrated by the author.
PRENTICE-HALL.

Watercolor and felt-tip pen over graphite

Strega Nona leaves Big Anthony alone with her magic pasta pot after telling him never to touch it. It is not long before he does, and pasta literally flows through the town. Characters in medieval costumes of pastel, jewel-like colors add to the humor of the story.

1975 AWARD

Arrow to the Sun: A Pueblo Indian Tale by Gerald McDermott, adapted and illustrated by the author. VIKING.

Gouache and ink; black line preseparated

The son of the Lord of the Sun sets out to find his father in this adaptation of a Pueblo legend. On his way, he undergoes four trials to prove his relationship to the Sun. The stylized, strong geometric art vividly portrays the desert and its intense sun colors.

HONOR

Jambo Means Hello: Swahili Alphabet Book **by Muriel Feelings, illustrated by Tom Feelings.** DIAL.

Graphite and paper collage

Letters of the alphabet are represented by words of the Swahili language. A brief explanation of the word includes cultural information of East African countries. Beautiful full-page illustrations further depict the cultures.

1974 AWARD

Duffy and the Devil: A Cornish Tale, **retold by Harve Zemach, illustrated by Margot Zemach.** FARRAR STRAUS GIROUX.

Pen-and-ink drawings with watercolor

The Cornish version of Rumpelstiltskin has delightful twists. When the maid guesses the devil's name, everything that he has sewn turns to ashes. Lightly colored illustrations treat the story with grand humor, and at the instant the name is guessed, the Squire is left standing in the fields, naked except for hat and shoes.

HONORS

Three Jovial Huntsmen, **adapted and illustrated by Susan Jeffers.** BRADBURY.

Pen-and-ink drawings with wash overlays painted in oils

The three jovial huntsmen go a-hunting on St. David's day and find nothing they want. But lurking in the beautifully drawn forests, many animals are seen keeping a close watch on the huntsmen.

Cathedral: The Story of Its Construction **by David Macaulay, illustrated by the author.** HOUGHTON MIFFLIN.

Pen and ink

The single-mindedness and spirit of the people and their step-by-step construction of an imaginary medieval cathedral are meticulously recorded as the author-illustrator celebrates the lives and art of the craftsmen who built the magnificent Gothic cathedrals.

1973 AWARD

The Funny Little Woman, **retold by Arlene Mosel, illustrated by Blair Lent.** DUTTON.

Pen-and-ink line drawings with full-color acrylic glazes; full-color paintings

A little woman pursues a rice dumpling and is led into the underground world of the wicked Oni. Her escape proves she is a funny little woman. Illustrations convey the mystery and humor of the strange world of the Oni as well as the dignity of this Japanese folktale.

HONORS

Hosie's Alphabet **by Hosea, Tobias, and Lisa Baskin, illustrated by Leonard Baskin. VIKING.**

Watercolor

From the bumptious baboon, to the primordial protozoa, right down to the "ruminating zebu," the artist presents an alphabet bestiary of ever-changing format where spiders' legs stretch across the page and dashes of watercolor become the eagle. This work is highly imaginative.

When Clay Sings **by Byrd Baylor, illustrated by Tom Bahti. SCRIBNER.**

Medium not known

Illustrated with the designs found on prehistoric pottery from the American Southwest, this tribute to artifacts and those who used them evokes a reverence for an ancient way of life. The earth tones and prehistoric designs dignify the word images of the poetic text.

Snow-White and the Seven Dwarfs: A Tale from the Brothers Grimm, **translated by Randall Jarrell, illustrated by Nancy Ekholm Burkert. FARRAR STRAUS GIROUX.**

Brush and colored inks

Strongly detailed illustrations in beautiful, soft colors evoke the sweeping, medieval, magical romance of fairy tales. Randall Jarrell translated the Brothers Grimm story of the beautiful girl, the wicked, malicious stepmother, and the sturdy, somber dwarfs.

Anansi the Spider: A Tale from the Ashanti, **adapted and illustrated by Gerald McDermott. HOLT RINEHART & WINSTON.**

Artwork preseparated in four colors with outline in ink

The moon is in the sky because Anansi, the great African folklore hero, could not decide which of his six sons should have it. Bright, geometric designs, bold, stylized animals, and rhythmic speech patterns are based on the Ashanti culture.

1972 AWARD

One Fine Day, **retold and illustrated by Nonny Hogrogian. MACMILLAN.**

Acrylic paintings with turpentine on gesso panels

Punished by having his tail cut off when he drank all the milk in an old woman's pail, the fox pleads to have it sewn back on so his friends won't make fun of him. The old woman agrees to do it, but only after he has returned her milk. The subdued and uncluttered pictures reflect the humorous cumulative action of the Armenian tale.

HONORS

If All the Seas Were One Sea by Janina Domanska, illustrated by the author. MACMILLAN.

Etchings on zinc plates with brush-and-ink overlays

An old nursery rhyme, its rise-and-fall rhythmic text reminiscent of the action of ocean waves, is treated to splendid etchings boldly filled with swirling, geometric lines of clear colors. The many shapes of each etching make a whole picture and provide the rhyme with even more momentum.

Moja Means One: Swahili Counting Book by Muriel Feelings, illustrated by Tom Feelings. DIAL.

Graphite and paper collage

Numbers from one to ten are represented by words in the Swahili language. Handsome, muted-gray double-page spread paintings depict scenes from Africa and relate to the illustrative sentences.

Hildilid's Night by Cheli Durán Ryan, illustrated by Arnold Lobel. MACMILLAN.

Pen-and-ink drawings with yellow overlays

Hildilid hates the night and the creatures of it. She does everything she can to chase the night away. Pen-and-ink drawings composed of thousands of tiny lines add a moonlit quality to the pages. Only at the end, with the approach of dawn, does yellow come into the picture.

1971 AWARD

A Story a Story: An African Tale, retold and illustrated by Gail E. Haley. ATHENEUM.

Woodcuts

Kwaku Ananse, the great African spider man, completes three almost impossible tasks to win the Sky God's box of stories to tell throughout the world. The woodcut illustrations use African designs.

HONORS

Frog and Toad Are Friends by Arnold Lobel, illustrated by the author. HARPER & ROW.

Pencil drawings in three colors

In five affectionate and funny stories, best friends Frog and Toad share simple adventures and experiences. They welcome spring, find a lost button, tell stories, and enjoy being friends. The expressive and droll illustrations are in gray, frog green, and toad brown.

In the Night Kitchen by Maurice Sendak, illustrated by the author. HARPER & ROW.

Line drawings and wash

Falling through the night and out of his clothes, Mickey lands in cake batter in the night kitchen. From there he goes to the dough, builds an airplane of it, and flies to the Milky Way. The dream-fantasy is carried out in a chanting rhyme and is illustrated with an adaptation of comic book art.

The Angry Moon, retold by William Sleator, illustrated by Blair Lent. ATLANTIC/LITTLE, BROWN.

Pen-and-ink drawings with acrylic glazes; full-color paintings

A legend of the peoples of Alaska is retold with vigor, using lavish, full-color illustrations that elaborate on original Tlingit motifs. When Lapowinsa mocks the moon, she is taken into the sky country. Her friend must overcome many obstacles before he is able to rescue her.

1970 AWARD

Sylvester and the Magic Pebble by William Steig, illustrated by the author. WINDMILL/SIMON & SCHUSTER.

Watercolor

A collector of pebbles, Sylvester the donkey finds a magic one that grants wishes. Caught by a lion, Sylvester panics and wishes himself to be a rock. Full-color pictures show the seasonal changes and colorful characters of the story and extend its concern and gentle humor.

HONORS

Goggles! by Ezra Jack Keats, illustrated by the author. MACMILLAN.

Oil paint and collage

While showing off the motorcycle goggles he has found, Peter is accosted by neighborhood bullies. Proving that smart moves are more powerful than brute strength, Peter and his friends outwit the older boys. Rich, dark, brooding colors of paint and collage are lightened with vibrant colors in illustrations that reflect the urban setting.

Alexander and the Wind-Up Mouse **by Leo Lionni, illustrated by the author. PANTHEON.**

Collage

Alexander, an unappreciated house mouse, envies Willy the windup mouse because everyone loves and coddles him. After asking the wizard lizard to change him into a windup mouse, Alexander has a change of heart. Large, bold collages enhance the simply told story.

Pop Corn and Ma Goodness **by Edna Mitchell Preston, illustrated by Robert Andrew Parker. VIKING.**

Watercolor

With all the gaiety and drama of a folk song, this original story is told in nonsense verse. Ma Goodness and Pop Corn meet, fall in love, marry, build a house and a farm, have children, and enjoy the good life on their "prippitty proppetty." Watercolor pictures have a haphazard look that adds to the rollicking fun.

Thy Friend, Obadiah **by Brinton Turkle, illustrated by the author. VIKING.**

Medium not known

His large Quaker family teases young Obadiah because a sea gull has taken a liking to him and follows him everywhere. The drawings are warm and gentle and vary greatly in perspective. When the sea gull fails to be seen for several days, Obadiah finds that what he thought was a nuisance is really a friend.

The Judge: An Untrue Tale **by Harve Zemach, illustrated by Margot Zemach. FARRAR STRAUS GIROUX.**

Watercolor, pen and ink

Prisoner after prisoner excitedly tells the Judge about the horrible thing that is on its way. The no-nonsense Judge throws them all in jail. When the horrible thing comes, poetic justice is done. Illustrated in watercolors and line drawings, the robust, pinkish characters tell their cumulative rhyming tale.

1969 AWARD

The Fool of the World and the Flying Ship: A Russian Tale, **retold by Arthur Ransome, illustrated by Uri Shulevitz. FARRAR STRAUS GIROUX.**

Pen and brush with black and colored inks

Line drawings and watercolors in bright, glowing, jewel-toned colors show the magnificent flying ship and the landscapes and onion domes of Russia. In this old Russian tale, the scorned and foolish younger son of peasants overcomes tremendous obstacles and wins the hand of the czar's daughter.

HONOR

Why the Sun and the Moon Live in the Sky by Elphinstone Dayrell, illustrated by Blair Lent. HOUGHTON MIFFLIN.

Preseparated pen and ink in three colors

Long ago, so the Nigerian folktale says, the Sun and Water were friends and lived on Earth together. When Sun invites Water to visit, the resulting flood forces them into the sky. Elaborately stylized African motifs and traditional patterns are used throughout the book.

1968 AWARD

Drummer Hoff, adapted by Barbara Emberley, illustrated by Ed Emberley. PRENTICE-HALL.

Woodcuts and ink

"Private Parridge brought the carriage," begins the cumulative text that leads to "Drummer Hoff fired it off" and a big "Kahbahblooom." Woodcuts show vibrantly colored old-fashioned military figures.

HONORS

Frederick by Leo Lionni, illustrated by the author. PANTHEON.

Collage with mixed media

The other field mice scurry to gather food for winter while Frederick gathers warm thoughts. In the deep of winter when the food has run out, Frederick is called upon to share his supplies. Collages enhance this story that proves "we do not live by bread alone."

Seashore Story by Taro Yashima, illustrated by the author. VIKING.

Watercolor and pastel

On an island where "the quietness of ancient times" is felt, visiting children are reminded of the old story of Urashima, a fisherman who saved the life of a turtle. In return, the turtle takes him deep into the ocean to a mythical land. Muted pastel drawings capture the mysticism of the Japanese story.

The Emperor and the Kite by Jane Yolen, illustrated by Ed Young. WORLD.

Paper cuts

Djeow Seow was the smallest and least noticed of the emperor's children. When evil men come and snatch the emperor away, it is Djeow Seow with her kites who rescues him. Intricate paper cuttings provide great beauty and a sense of cultural heritage in this Japanese tale.

1967 AWARD

Sam, Bangs & Moonshine by Evaline Ness, illustrated by the author.
HOLT RINEHART & WINSTON.

Three-color preseparated art using Japanese pen and wash; printer's ink; roller; string

Sam, a fisherman's daughter, has a bad habit of making up stories. The little girl learns to distinguish the truth from "moonshine" only after her best friend and her cat nearly meet tragedy. The book's pictures capture Sam's confusion of fact and fancy.

HONOR

One Wide River to Cross, adapted by Barbara Emberley, illustrated by
Ed Emberley. PRENTICE-HALL.

Woodcuts

The text of an old folk song comes alive on brightly colored pages printed with black woodcuts. Stylized animals come forth one by one, two by two, and so on up to ten in nonsense verse with illustrations of animals that cumulate in groups waiting to board Noah's ark.

1966 AWARD

Always Room for One More by Sorche Nic Leodhas, pseud. (Leclaire Alger),
illustrated by Nonny Hogrogian. HOLT RINEHART & WINSTON.

Three-color preseparated art using pen for black line and pastels and wash for color

A man invites all passersby to share his house with his wife and ten children until the house finally bursts apart. The Scottish folk song is told in lilting verse and illustrated in a subdued, dreamy manner.

HONORS

Just Me by Marie Hall Ets, illustrated by the author. VIKING.

Paper batik

The little boy tries to imitate the hops, walks, and wiggles of the animals on his farm. But when he sees his father, he runs to him as only he can run. Black-and-white drawings have a charming rhythmic expression.

Tom Tit Tot, retold and illustrated by Evaline Ness. SCRIBNER.

Woodcuts

In this English variant of Rumpelstiltskin, the heroine is a comic, homespun character. Woodcuts executed in brown, gold, black, and aqua capture the broad humor and Elizabethan tone of the story.

Hide and Seek Fog by Alvin Tresselt, illustrated by Roger Duvoisin. LOTHROP.

Full-color gouache

As thick fog settles down for a stay, the lobstermen cannot put out to sea, the vacationers grumble because they cannot do anything, and the children frolic and play hide-and-seek. Pictures and text describe how life becomes transformed in a dense, wet, lingering fog on the Atlantic seacoast.

1965 AWARD

May I Bring a Friend? by Beatrice Schenk de Regniers, illustrated by
Beni Montresor. ATHENEUM.

Pen-and-ink drawings on board in black with solid overlays and screened overlays on acetate

Invited to tea by the king and queen each day of one week, the child quite naturally asks if he can bring a friend with him. Each day he brings animals from the zoo, and not all are well behaved! In rhymed text and creative illustrations reminiscent of stage settings, the absurd story is told.

HONORS

A Pocketful of Cricket by Rebecca Caudill, illustrated by Evaline Ness.
HOLT RINEHART & WINSTON.

Medium not known

One day a boy who delights in the countryside finds a cricket and takes it home for a pet. An understanding teacher shows him how to share his special love of the cricket with the whole class. Pictures portray the inquisitiveness of a young farm boy.

The Wave by Margaret Hodges, adapted from Lafacdio Hearn's *Gleanings in Buddha-Fields*, illustrated by Blair Lent. HOUGHTON MIFFLIN.

Ink and cardboard cutouts

Giisan, the wise and respected old man of the Japanese village, must act quickly to warn the villagers that they are in great danger. The relentlessness of the tidal wave is seen in the brown, gold, gray, and black prints on every page and is heard in the urgency with which the story is told.

Rain Makes Applesauce by Julian Scheer, illustrated by Marvin Bileck.
HOLIDAY HOUSE.

Pencil and watercolors (?)

Each two-page spread contains a nonsense line that always ends with "And rain makes applesauce" and the accusation, "Oh you're just talking silly talk." Illustrations in rich but delicate colors have an almost surrealistic effect and add a sophisticated tone.

1964 AWARD

Where the Wild Things Are by Maurice Sendak, illustrated by the author.
HARPER & ROW.

India ink line over full-color tempera

Sent to bed without any supper, Max travels far to where the wild things are. Taming them with a special magic trick, Max suddenly longs to be at home. The pictures are full of movement and magic, and in several two-page spreads without text they are absolutely boisterous.

HONORS

Swimmy by Leo Lionni, illustrated by the author. PANTHEON.

Watercolor, rubber stamping, and pencil

Swimmy, a small, black fish, convinces a school of small fish to swim in the formation of a large fish, thus proving that in numbers there is strength. The watery world is filled with shapes, patterns, and colors.

All in the Morning Early by Sorche Nic Leodhas, pseud. (Leclaire Alger), illustrated by Evaline Ness. HOLT RINEHART & WINSTON.

Medium not known

Asked by his mother to take a sack of corn to the mill, Sandy starts on his way. With each animal or person he meets along the way, the cumulative rhythmic tale grows longer. The drawings, with their overlapping colors, place the scene in Scotland, where the old rhyme originated.

Mother Goose and Nursery Rhymes, illustrated by Philip Reed. ATHENEUM.

Engravings on wood

Wood engravings, both serious and silly in approach, decorate nearly all sixty-six rhymes and proverbs included in this collection. Large print, generous margins, crisp and colorful engravings, and just one or two nursery rhymes a page encourage a lingering look at each illustration.

1963 AWARD

The Snowy Day by Ezra Jack Keats, illustrated by the author. VIKING.

Collage: papers, paints, and gum-eraser stamps

Peter has fun on a snow-covered day making tracks and angels in the snow, building a snowman, and even trying to save a snowball for later. Spare, colorful collage pictures capture the wonder of a small child's trudge through new snow.

HONORS

The Sun Is a Golden Earring by Natalia M. Belting, illustrated by
Bernarda Bryson. HOLT RINEHART & WINSTON.

Pencil

People have always wondered about nature and have made up stories and sayings to
explain natural phenomena. The author's collection of ancient sayings from folklore is
reproduced here. The drawings lend an effective ethereal spirit to the book.

Mr. Rabbit and the Lovely Present by Charlotte Zolotow, illustrated by
Maurice Sendak. HARPER & ROW.

Watercolor

A little girl seeks birthday present advice from the wonderfully lanky, long-legged
Mr. Rabbit. As the two wander through beautiful pastel scenes, she explains that her
mother likes colors. They discuss many objects that are of the colors her mother likes
the best.

1962 AWARD

Once a Mouse . . . A Fable, retold and illustrated by Marcia Brown. SCRIBNER.

Woodcuts and watercolor

The brief, carefully chosen text taken from a fable of ancient India tells of a hermit
magician that changes a mouse into a cat, a dog, a tiger, and finally back into a mouse
again. Illustrated in woodcuts filled with patterns, the overlaying of the gold, red, and
black add even more dimension.

HONORS

The Day We Saw the Sun Come Up by Alice E. Goudey, illustrated by
Adrienne Adams. SCRIBNER.

Graphite and gray wash with white gouache separations

In this poetic science book, two children get up very early in the morning and see the
sun come up. They watch their long shadows and see what happens to them later in
the day. Illustrations are in appropriate colors—gray and shadowy in the early morning, bright and clear at noon.

Little Bear's Visit by Else Holmelund Minarik, illustrated by
Maurice Sendak. HARPER.

Pen and ink with wash separations

Little Bear thoroughly enjoys his visit with his grandparents and delights in the stories they tell. The brown, green, and black-and-white illustrations of the cuddly, loving
Little Bear and his fully clothed grandparents are enhanced with fine crosshatching.

The Fox Went Out on a Chilly Night: An Old Song, **illustrated by Peter Spier.** DOUBLEDAY.

Pen and ink and watercolor on blue boards

Alternating double-page spreads of full-color and black-and-white detailed drawings greatly extend the story told in the old song. The fox kills a duck and a goose, outruns the farmer, and dines with his wife with fork and knife while the ten little pups chew on the "bones-o." The musical score is appended.

1961 AWARD

Baboushka and the Three Kings, **adapted from a Russian folk tale by Ruth Robbins, illustrated by Nicolas Sidjakov.** PARNASSUS.

Tempera and felt-tip pen in four colors

Old Baboushka declined to go with the three kings in search of the Child. Now, every year at Christmastime she continues her endless, endless search. On her way she leaves gifts for children. Rich, four-color, angular pictures in primitive style adorn the Russian tale.

HONOR

Inch by Inch **by Leo Lionni, illustrated by the author.** OBOLENSKY.

Rice paper collage and crayon

An inchworm saves himself from being eaten because he is able to measure things—a robin's tail, a flamingo's neck, a hummingbird's body. But when asked to measure the nightingale's song, the inchworm must think fast. The bright green inchworm inches its way out of sight through a collage of grass.

1960 AWARD

Nine Days to Christmas **by Marie Hall Ets and Aurora Labastida, illustrated by Marie Hall Ets.** VIKING.

Pencil on Dinobase

Now that she is in kindergarten, Ceci is old enough to join in the posadas—part of the special Christmas celebration that begins nine days before Christmas. Anticipation mounts as Ceci chooses her own piñata. Soft, gray backgrounds with splashes of bright colors project the warmth and excitement of the Mexican tradition in an urban setting.

HONORS

Houses from the Sea by Alice E. Goudey, illustrated by
Adrienne Adams. SCRIBNER.

Watercolor (?)

Soft watercolor washes combine with poetic text to set the tone of this quiet, informative story. Two children gather shells along the coast and talk about the various shapes of the shells. An introduction and afterword provide more scientific information.

The Moon Jumpers by Janice May Udry, illustrated by Maurice Sendak. HARPER.

Tempera

When the sun goes down, the moon comes up. Four children calling themselves the moon jumpers joyfully play and dance under the moonlit sky before bedtime. Soft night colors add a mystic touch to the simple story.

1959 AWARD

Chanticleer and the Fox by Geoffrey Chaucer, adapted and illustrated by
Barbara Cooney. CROWELL.

Preseparated art: black and white on scratchboard; colors on Dinobase

The old fable of the proud rooster and the wily fox was retold by Chaucer in his *Canterbury Tales.* Cooney has adapted that version for children. The text is filled with descriptive language, while the illustrations, rich in color and strong lines, capture medieval times.

HONORS

The House That Jack Built/La Maison Que Jacques A Batie by Antonio Frasconi,
illustrated by the author. HARCOURT BRACE.

Woodcuts

An old cumulative nursery rhyme, told in English and French, is illustrated with brilliantly colored woodcuts. A review at the end of the text asks questions in English and provides answers in French.

What Do You Say, Dear? by Sesyle Joslin, illustrated by Maurice Sendak.
YOUNG SCOTT.

Pen and ink with watercolor wash separations

Absurdly funny and outlandish situations are presented, followed by the question, "what do you say, dear?" and the proper rule of etiquette. Blue, yellow, and black illustrations continue the hilarity, even though the rule is presented straightforwardly.

Umbrella by Taro Yashima, illustrated by the author. VIKING.

Watercolor; pencil and brush for direct separations

Thrilled with the umbrella and red boots she receives on her third birthday, Momo impatiently waits out the days until it rains. How proud she is when she can finally use her new rain gear! The impressionistic illustrations are filled with brush strokes of red, blues, and yellows and reflect the Japanese culture.

1958 AWARD

Time of Wonder by Robert McCloskey, illustrated by the author. VIKING.

Casein

McCloskey celebrates in prose and painting the island where he lives. The alternately quiet and boisterous moods of nature are peacefully or dramatically recounted. The children of the island explore and enjoy the changing moods as the intensity of the blue and green watercolors shifts with the changes in the weather.

HONORS

Fly High, Fly Low by Don Freeman, illustrated by the author. VIKING.

Colored pencil accented by outlines in ink

In a story of love, loyalty, and suspense, the pigeon Sid faces perils while searching for the missing Midge, their nest, and the big letter B where their nest is housed. Colorful illustrations reveal scenes of San Francisco.

Anatole and the Cat by Eve Titus, illustrated by Paul Galdone. McGRAW-HILL.

Pen and ink with gray wash over graphite with paper collage (?)

Mouse Anatole, a loving husband and caring father, bicycles through the streets of Paris each night on his way to work. When a cat arrives on the scene, Anatole succeeds where thousands of other mice have failed. Gray drawings with accents of red, white, and blue and a smattering of French words reinforce the setting of the story.

1957 AWARD

A Tree Is Nice by Janice May Udry, illustrated by Marc Simont. HARPER.

Gouache over watercolor

Trees are wonderful: They give shade, are fun to climb, are great to swing from, and even give cats a place to hide from dogs. Illustrated with watercolors, this book is a celebration of trees.

HONORS

Gillespie and the Guards by Benjamin Elkin, illustrated by James Daugherty. VIKING.

Charcoal rubbed off on light gray transfer and inked (?)

Gillespie sets out to fool the three haughty guards by the old trick of the obvious. Robust illustrations are filled with humor and point with pride to the little boy who outsmarts the smug guards.

Lion by William Pène du Bois, illustrated by the author. VIKING.

Pen and india ink; color preseparated on Dinobase with lithographic pencil

High in the sky, in the place where animals are invented, the boss comes up with a wonderful new name for an animal—"lion." His difficulty in deciding what it should look like is depicted in a line drawing of his original idea of a lion, complete with feathers, fur, and fish scales.

Mr. Penny's Race Horse by Marie Hall Ets, illustrated by the author. VIKING.

Paper batik

Mr. Penny promises his animals a ride on the Ferris wheel if they win enough prize money at the fair. In an attempt to make sure they win first prize, the animals cause chaos. The dark black-and-white illustrations of the farm and the fair are all set within a border.

Anatole by Eve Titus, illustrated by Paul Galdone. McGRAW-HILL.

Pen and ink with gray wash over graphite with paper collage (?)

Shocked and shaken when he overhears humans saying that mice are terrible and dirty, Anatole the mouse determines to give humans something in return for the food he takes. Red, white, blue, and gray illustrations alternate with black-and-white ones as they reveal the world from the perspective of a French mouse.

1 Is One by Tasha Tudor, illustrated by the author. OXFORD.

Graphite and watercolor (?)

Simple verse and delicate old-fashioned paintings and drawings introduce numerals from one to twenty. Each page is bordered with charming drawings of wild flowers. Within the borders children and scenes from nature represent the number depicted.

1956 AWARD

Frog Went A-Courtin', retold by John Langstaff, illustrated by Feodor Rojankovsky. HARCOURT BRACE.

Brush, ink, and crayon on acetate separations

In this story based on an old song and written in snappy, rhyming couplets, a frog courts Miss Mousie, and soon the insects and small animals scurry about preparing for the wedding feast. Full-color illustrations alternate with black-and-white and frog green ones, climaxing in a state of confusion as the cat joins the feast. Music is included.

HONORS

Play with Me **by Marie Hall Ets, illustrated by the author.** VIKING.

Graphite separations

Reaching out to touch the woodland animals that she wants to play with, the little girl finds that they all run from her. She sits very still, and one by one the animals come close to her. Repetition in the story is loosely carried out in the quiet drawings as the girl never strays far from the pond.

Crow Boy **by Taro Yashima, illustrated by the author.** VIKING.

Pencil and brush separations

In a deeply sensitive school story, Chibi, a very shy boy, is taunted by his classmates for years. A new teacher takes the time to talk to Chibi and discovers his talents. Set in a Japanese village, the story is illustrated with brush strokes that reflect an economy of style.

1955 AWARD

Cinderella, or the Little Glass Slipper **by Charles Perrault, translated and illustrated by Marcia Brown.** SCRIBNER.

Gouache, crayon, watercolor, and ink

Freely translated from Charles Perrault's French tale, this story of Cinderella, her ugly stepsisters, the fairy godmother, and the glass slipper is enhanced with illustrations that fairly dance across the pages with pink and aqua colors and whispy black lines. The enchanting pictures capture the romance of the tale.

HONORS

Wheel on the Chimney **by Margaret Wise Brown, illustrated by Tibor Gergely.** LIPPINCOTT.

Gouache (?)

Storks come from Africa to build their nest on the chimney and live by the cool, green rivers of Hungary. When fall comes they fly south over towns, rivers, and bridges. The full-page paintings of the Mediterranean city, the pink flamingos, and the flock of white storks in flight are striking in color.

The Thanksgiving Story by Alice Dalgliesh, illustrated by Helen Sewell. SCRIBNER.

Medium not known

Events leading up to the first Thanksgiving celebration in Plymouth Colony are told with the Hopkins family as the focus. Flat, primitive color illustrations of people are interspersed with rust-colored silhouettes of objects important to the Pilgrims in their new land.

Book of Nursery and Mother Goose Rhymes, illustrated by Marguerite de Angeli. DOUBLEDAY.

Sharp Wolf pencils and watercolor

Three hundred seventy-six rhymes are delicately illustrated in this oversized book. A soft, cheerful tone pervades the sketches, many of which were inspired by scenes of the English countryside. A small sketch of a goose appears on almost every page.

1954 AWARD

Madeline's Rescue by Ludwig Bemelmans, illustrated by the author. VIKING.

Brush, pen, and watercolor

When Madeline is rescued from the river by a dog, the dog becomes the heroine of the convent school. The girls love the dog, but the trustees say it must go. Bright, irrepressible pictures match the indomitable spirit of the little French girl.

HONORS

The Steadfast Tin Soldier by Hans Christian Andersen, translated by M. R. James, illustrated by Marcia Brown. SCRIBNER.

Medium not known

Five-and-twenty tin soldiers, all made from the same tin spoon, look alike except for the last one made. He stands firmly on his one leg. It is he who falls in love with the toy ballerina. Their tragic story is enhanced with blue-violet and red drawings.

Green Eyes by Abe Birnbaum, illustrated by the author. CAPITOL.

Medium not known

An all-white cat with long whiskers and green eyes is about to celebrate his first birthday. In simple text and drawings reminiscent of the bold lines of children's art, the tale of Green Eyes's activities in the four seasons that have just passed unfolds.

A Very Special House by Ruth Krauss, illustrated by Maurice Sendak. HARPER.

Medium not known

The little boy is blissfully happy as he tells of a house he knows where he puts his feet on the table, bounces on the bed, and swings on the door. It is a place where everyone yells for more, and no one ever says "stop." Line illustrations seem to frolic across the page, and only at the end is it revealed that the story is a triumph of imaginary play.

Journey Cake, Ho! by Ruth Sawyer, illustrated by Robert McCloskey. VIKING.

Medium not known

When there is only enough food left to feed two, not three, the bound-out boy is sent on his way with a huge Journey Cake. The cake breaks free, bounces down the road, and soon animal after animal joins the chase until they all end up where the boy started. Expressive illustrations provide the feel of an American folktale.

When Will the World Be Mine? The Story of a Snowshoe Rabbit by Miriam Schlein, illustrated by Jean Charlot. W. R. SCOTT.

Lithographs (?)

Little Snowshoe Rabbit is born in the spring. His mother spends much of the year protecting and teaching him. She gently shows him how to adapt to the world around him, and in that way the world becomes his. The lithographs in browns and greens show stylized rabbits and their view of the world.

1953 AWARD

The Biggest Bear by Lynd Ward, illustrated by the author. HOUGHTON MIFFLIN.

Wood engraving

Humiliated because his family has the only barn that never has a bear skin hanging on it, Johnny sets out with his shotgun in search of a bear. He returns home with a live, cuddly, hungry bear cub that soon grows into a big, rambunctious, voracious bear. The illustrations are sensitive, strong, and robust.

HONORS

Ape in a Cape: An Alphabet of Odd Animals by Fritz Eichenberg, illustrated by the author. HARCOURT BRACE.

Woodcuts; acetate separations

Bold, humorous, colorful pictures and short, nonsense verses combine to create a lively alphabet book. From the "bear in despair" to the "yak with a pack," there is wonderful fun and imagination on each page.

Five Little Monkeys by Juliet Kepes, illustrated by the author. HOUGHTON MIFFLIN.

Preseparated ink and watercolor wash (four-color)

Buzzo, Binki, Bulu, Bibi, and Bali are the little mischievous monkeys who, because of their irritating tricks, cause the other jungle animals to band together to punish them. Alternating pages of color and black-and-white illustrations show the stylized monkeys acting up.

One Morning in Maine by Robert McCloskey, illustrated by the author. VIKING.

Lithographs (?)

While clam digging with her father, Sally loses a tooth that falls amongst the pebbles of the beach. Large, dark blue lithographs depict the great pride associated with losing the first baby tooth. All the characters in the small Maine town enjoy Sally's joy.

Puss in Boots by Charles Perrault, translated and illustrated by Marcia Brown. SCRIBNER.

Woodcut and watercolor (?)

The youngest son inherits a cat and realizes that after eating it he will have nothing left. Crafty Puss in Boots tells his master to do as he says and all will be well, and indeed it is! Puss, with his fine red boots, is shown as a grand, swashbuckling character who takes command of all the folderol of a French court.

The Storm Book by Charlotte Zolotow, illustrated by Margaret Bloy Graham. HARPER.

Medium not known

A little boy watches in wonder as the day turns ominously gray and still, a storm approaches, and breaks forth. He asks his mother questions and she replies with reassuring answers. Each two-page spread of text is followed by a double-page spread of illustrations, most of them showing a driving rain.

1952 AWARD

Finders Keepers by Will, pseud. (William Lipkind), illustrated by Nicolas, pseud. (Nicolas Mordvinoff). HARCOURT BRACE.

Acetate color separations for line reproduction

Two dogs find a bone. One saw it first; the other touched it first. Unable to decide who owns it, they bury it and go off to seek the opinion of others and in so doing almost lose the bone to another dog. The bold use of color adds spark and flair to the simple story.

HONORS

Skipper John's Cook by Marcia Brown, illustrated by the author. SCRIBNER.

Medium not known

Beans! That was the trouble. The Skipper's crew refuses to sign on until a cook is found who does not fix beans morning, noon, and night. Young Si is hired on. After he has fried his 259th fish, the crew wants to know what else he can cook. Beans! Illustrations capture the expressions of the crew—and of the pots and pans.

Bear Party by William Pène du Bois, illustrated by the author. VIKING.

Medium not known

When the koala bears become very angry with each other, it is "the wise old bear who lives at the top of the tallest Eucalyptus tree" who decides what to do. The koala bears are shown dressed in all the finery of a masked costume party, while wonderful onomatopoeic words describe the sounds of the musical instruments.

Mr. T. W. Anthony Woo by Marie Hall Ets, illustrated by the author. VIKING.

Paper batik

Pandemonium reigns at the cobbler's when his dog and cat fight each other, and then both chase Mr. T. W. Anthony Woo, the mouse. Sister and her parrot move in, and things go from bad to worse until the enemies band together to create peace. Illustrations are contained within borders and suggest the control the cobbler wishes he had.

Feather Mountain by Elizabeth Olds, illustrated by the author. HOUGHTON MIFFLIN.

Preseparated art and watercolor wash (four-color)

At one time all birds were naked and pink and featherless. One day they ask the Great Spirit to give them coverings. Black-and-white and color pictures depict the birds as they scurry around finding just the right colors to blend with their habitats.

All Falling Down by Gene Zion, illustrated by Margaret Bloy Graham. HARPER.

Medium not known

So many things fall—petals, rain, apples, even Daddy's book when his head begins to nod. This quiet, reflective book is illustrated with pastel colors. There is a surprise ending when Daddy tosses the baby in the air.

1951 AWARD

The Egg Tree by Katherine Milhous, illustrated by the author. SCRIBNER.

Tempera

An Easter morning egg hunt leads to the discovery of long forgotten decorated eggs. With them the family begins a new tradition. Pennsylvania Dutch folk designs border many of the pages; the colors found in hex signs dominate the paintings that interpret the story.

HONORS

Dick Whittington and His Cat by Marcia Brown, illustrated by the author. SCRIBNER.

Linoleum cuts

Artistic linoleum block cuts have humor and charm. They illustrate a simple retelling of the folktale of the boy who was made wealthy because he listened to his cat.

If I Ran the Zoo by Dr. Seuss, pseud. (Theodor Seuss Geisel), illustrated by the author. RANDOM HOUSE.

Pencil, ink, and watercolor

Young Gerald McGrew likes the zoo but knows that if he ran it he would make some changes. He imagines all kinds of fantastic beasts with wonderfully creative names and unusual shapes and habits. Zany, whimsical illustrations are perfect for the imaginative verse.

The Two Reds by Will, pseud. (William Lipkind), illustrated by Nicolas, pseud. (Nicolas Mordvinoff). HARCOURT BRACE.

Acetate separations using pen, ink, and brush

Red, the boy, sets out to play at the same time Red, an independent cat, sets out for food. The sense of impending chaos mounts as each gets in trouble at the same time in different parts of town. Sparse line drawings with brilliant splashes of red add spark to the illustrations.

T-Bone, the Baby Sitter by Clare Turlay Newberry, illustrated by the author. HARPER.

Pen, ink, and charcoal (?)

T-Bone the cat loves to sit. That is what makes him such a fine babysitter—until the day he awakens with a twinkle in his eye, full of mischief. Expressive illustrations show the baby's extreme displeasure when T-Bone is taken away to the country and his pleasure when he returns.

The Most Wonderful Doll in the World by Phyllis McGinley, illustrated by Helen Stone. LIPPINCOTT.

Medium not known

Duley loses a new doll. Her imagination runs wild as she describes the lost and most wonderful doll in the world as she wants it to be, not as it is. The book is decorated with four-color and black-and-white illustrations and borders.

1950 AWARD

Song of the Swallows by **Leo Politi, illustrated by the author. SCRIBNER.**

Tempera

The bell ringer and gardener of the mission church in Capistrano tells Juan the history of the mission churches and of the return of the swallows every St. Joseph's Day. Pinks, grays, yellows, and greens in muted tones convey friendship and a respect for nature. Two songs are included in the text.

HONORS

Henry—Fisherman by **Marcia Brown, illustrated by the author. SCRIBNER.**

Collage (?)

To be a fisherman a boy has to be able to swim very fast in case a shark is near. As the day when Juan will be allowed on the fishing boat draws closer, sights and sounds of a childhood in the Virgin Islands are portrayed in brown, coral, yellow, and green.

The Wild Birthday Cake by **Lavinia R. Davis, illustrated by Hildegard Woodward. DOUBLEDAY.**

Medium not known

Johnny is so excited about going on an adventurous hike that he almost forgets his friend's seventy-fifth birthday. On his hike he catches a wild duck and later gives it to his friend as a gift. Abundant on the pages are the yellows and greens of spring.

Bartholomew and the Oobleck by **Dr. Seuss, pseud. (Theodor Seuss Geisel), illustrated by the author. RANDOM HOUSE.**

Pencil, crayon, and watercolor

Tired of snow, fog, rain, and sunshine, the king wants something new to fall from the sky. What he gets are green, gooey globs of oobleck that threaten to destroy the kingdom. Comical illustrations in black-and-white become greener and greener as the oobleck spreads.

America's Ethan Allen by **Stewart Holbrook, illustrated by Lynd Ward. HOUGHTON MIFFLIN.**

Full-color gouache paintings

Brave and rebellious Ethan Allen is born in the wilds of the old colony of Connecticut. He grows into a rugged frontier hero who leads the Green Mountain Boys. The illustrations and writing style resound with patriotism and historical significance.

The Happy Day by Ruth Krauss, illustrated by Marc Simont. HARPER.

Medium not known

The woodland animals are all in their winter's sleep when something causes them to open their eyes and sniff. Suspense mounts as they all race toward the thing that has caused them to awaken. Black-and-white drawings portray joyous animals as they leap around a bright yellow flower—the first sign of spring and the only color in the book.

1949 AWARD

The Big Snow by Berta and Elmer Hader, illustrated by the authors. MACMILLAN.

Watercolor

When they see the wild geese flying overhead, all the woodland animals scurry to get ready for winter. After the big snow they slowly emerge to find food. Black-and-white drawings are occasionally interspersed with full-color paintings.

HONORS

Blueberries for Sal by Robert McCloskey, illustrated by the author. VIKING.

Lithographs (?)

On the same day that Little Sal and her mother go to Blueberry Hill to pick blueberries, so do Little Bear and his mother. Soon a mix-up in mothers occurs. Dark blue-and-white type and drawings promote gentle humor against the ruggedness of Blueberry Hill.

All around the Town by Phyllis McGinley, illustrated by Helen Stone. LIPPINCOTT.

Medium not known

Snappy rhythm of the text and splashes of color in the illustrations capture the gaiety and pace of city life. Each verse is about a city sight and the rhymes are arranged in alphabetical order, from Aeroplane to Zoo.

Juanita by Leo Politi, illustrated by the author. SCRIBNER.

Tempera (?)

As Easter draws near, Juanita and her friends join in the parade for the Blessing of the Animals at the Old Mission Church. The text is lovingly illustrated and interspersed with some songs, making the warmth of a close-knit community in old Los Angeles come alive.

Fish in the Air by Kurt Wiese, illustrated by the author. VIKING.

Ink and watercolor

On their way to fly a great big kite, Fish and his kite are grabbed by a Tai Fung, or big wind. It sends them on a high-flying adventure. Colorful paintings portray the excitement caused when Fish flies over town and countryside.

1948 AWARD

White Snow, Bright Snow by Alvin Tresselt, illustrated by
Roger Duvoisin. LOTHROP.

Acetate separations in india ink

Slowly the snow begins to fall and the adults busy themselves preparing for it. The children revel in it. A dark blue background gives way to white as the heavy snow melts and spring breaks forth. Reds and yellows provide a cheerful balance.

HONORS

Stone Soup: An Old Tale by Marcia Brown, illustrated by the author. SCRIBNER.

Ink and watercolor (?)

An inhospitable town refuses to help three hungry soldiers. When the soldiers decide to make a soup of stones, curiosity overcomes the peasants and they learn a lesson in cooperation. Orange and brown pictures portray peasant life in a long-ago French village.

Roger and the Fox by Lavinia R. Davis, illustrated by
Hildegard Woodward. DOUBLEDAY.

Ink (?)

Roger wants to see the wild fox and tries many times before he figures out how to be quick and quiet enough to do it. The pictures turn from the warm hues of fall to the cold blues of winter before patience and ingenuity finally pay off.

McElligot's Pool by Dr. Seuss, pseud. (Theodor Seuss Geisel), illustrated by
the author. RANDOM HOUSE.

Pencil and watercolor

Told that he is some sort of fool for trying to catch fish in McElligot's pool, Marco visualizes the possibility that the pool is connected to the sea. Wonderfully imaginative creatures with fantastic names swim across the pages of this story told in verse.

Song of Robin Hood, selected by Anne Malcolmson, music by Grace Castagnetta, designed and illustrated by Virginia Lee Burton. HOUGHTON MIFFLIN.

Scratchboard

Eighteen ballads of Robin Hood, most traced back to their original tunes, are exuberantly presented in verse, music, and art. The five hundred verses are decorated in a style reminiscent of miniature drawings of the fifteenth century. Its words meant to be sung not read, the book provides an energetic and lyrical introduction to the famous Robin Hood.

Bambino the Clown by Georges Schreiber, illustrated by the author. VIKING.

Medium not known

The full colors and excitement of a circus clown's act are experienced by a sad young boy whom Bambino befriends. Peter is invited into the clown's dressing room, watches him apply his makeup, and becomes a very funny part of the show.

1947 AWARD

The Little Island by Golden MacDonald, pseud. (Margaret Wise Brown), illustrated by Leonard Weisgard. DOUBLEDAY.

Gouache

The seasons come and go and little by little the small island changes. One day a kitten visits the island and discovers that it does not stand alone but is connected underwater to land. The moods of the mostly green and blue drawings change with the seasons.

HONORS

The Boats on the River by Marjorie Flack, illustrated by Jay Hyde Barnum. VIKING.

Medium not known

There are warships, ocean liners, rowboats, and many other boats on the river that flows by the city and out to sea. Full-color paintings show close and distant views of the boats.

Timothy Turtle by Al Graham, illustrated by Tony Palazzo. ROBERT WELCH.

Black-and-white pen and ink (?)

On the day Timothy flips over on his back, each animal tries to help him right himself. The wise frog tells the other animals that what they could not do as individuals they can do as a group. Action-packed drawings add tautness and humor to the tale.

Pedro, the Angel of Olvera Street by Leo Politi, illustrated by the author. SCRIBNER.

Medium not known

Young Pedro, who sings like an angel, leads La Posada, the Christmas procession, on Olvera Street in Los Angeles. For nine consecutive nights he wears red wings and sings carols of Christian pilgrims. The soft colors reflect the solemnity of the procession. Music is included.

Rain Drop Splash by Alvin Tresselt, illustrated by Leonard Weisgard. LOTHROP.

Three colors preseparated with india ink on acetate overlays

A single rain drop splashes down. Soon it is joined by others, and a puddle is formed. The puddle grows bigger and bigger until the rain drops at last become the sea, and the rain stops. The poetic patterns of the text and the drenched look of the pictures provide a closeness to nature.

Sing in Praise: A Collection of the Best Loved Hymns, stories and arrangements by Opal Wheeler, illustrated by Marjorie Torrey. DUTTON.

Medium not known

Twenty-five perennially popular Christian hymns have been arranged to simple piano scores. Most of the hymns are accompanied by a laudatory story about how the particular words or melody came to be written. Romanticized illustrations show pious children looking heavenward.

1946 AWARD

The Rooster Crows: A Book of American Rhymes and Jingles by Maud and Miska Petersham, illustrated by the authors. MACMILLAN.

Lithograph pencil with color separations on acetate

A potpourri of the rhymes, jingles, and chants of American children is treated to a variety of visual interpretations. Each rhyme is illustrated with humor and rhythm.

Published in a revised edition with new text and illustrations in 1966 (Macmillan).

HONORS

Little Lost Lamb by Golden MacDonald, pseud. (Margaret Wise Brown), illustrated by Leonard Weisgard. DOUBLEDAY.

Medium not known

When the little black lamb strays from the rest of the flock, the little shepherd and his sheepdog go into the perilous night in search of it. The mood of the story changes from bright, frolicsome pictures of the frisky lamb to dark browns that reflect the concern the boy has for the lost animal.

My Mother Is the Most Beautiful Woman in the World by Becky Reyher, illustrated by Ruth Chrisman Gannett. LOTHROP.

Original gouache and watercolor reproduced by four-match process using lithographic crayon

When a little girl becomes lost, she describes her mother with her heart not with her eyes. Colorful pictures reflect the spirit of the old Russian proverb, "We do not love people because they are beautiful, but they seem beautiful to us because we love them."

Sing Mother Goose, **music by Opal Wheeler, illustrated by Marjorie Torrey. DUTTON.**

Medium not known

Fifty-two of the most familiar Mother Goose nursery rhymes have been arranged to original, sprightly music. The piano scores and the rhymes are accompanied by illustrations of children, many of whom are in late-Victorian dress.

You Can Write Chinese **by Kurt Wiese, illustrated by the author. VIKING.**

Ink and watercolor separations

In China in the 1940s, a classroom of boys receives a language lesson. The teacher explains that there are no letters in the Chinese language, only words based on ancient pictures. Most of the book consists of large drawings of Chinese characters superimposed on drawings of objects that represent the words.

1945 AWARD

Prayer for a Child **by Rachel Field, illustrated by Elizabeth Orton Jones. MACMILLAN.**

Pen and ink; watercolor

A child's bedtime prayer asks for blessings on things that are familiar to small children with such lines as, "Bless other children, far and near, And keep them safe and free from fear." Brief lines of the prayer are illustrated with full-page, reverent golden-toned drawings.

HONORS

In the Forest **by Marie Hall Ets, illustrated by the author. VIKING.**

Paper batik

With his new horn and paper hat a little boy takes a walk in the forest, and along the way he meets storks, kangaroos, bears, and other animals who join his parade. All disappear when the boy's father comes hunting for him. There is a strong contrast between the white figures and the black forest backgrounds.

Yonie Wondernose **by Marguerite de Angeli, illustrated by the author. DOUBLEDAY.**

Color separations done in pen, ink, pencil, and watercolor

His father has promised him something very special as soon as seven-year-old Yonie learns to handle responsibilities like a man. Strongly depicted in the illustrations and the text is the hard but cheerful way of life on an Amish farm.

The Christmas Anna Angel by Ruth Sawyer, illustrated by Kate Seredy. VIKING.

Medium not known

In a story set in Hungary during the war, Anna longs for a Christmas cake shaped like a little clock. The deprivations caused by the war contrast with the happy family traditions of Christmas. While heavy on text, the book has several illustrations reflective of the folk culture.

Mother Goose: Seventy-seven Verses, illustrated by Tasha Tudor. OXFORD.

Graphite and watercolor (?)

Seventy-seven Mother Goose rhymes are gathered together in this small book. Many of the rhymes are familiar, but some are those usually found only in complete works. Quaint, soft-colored pictures abound on every page.

1944 AWARD

Many Moons by James Thurber, illustrated by Louis Slobodkin. HARCOURT BRACE.

Pen and ink; watercolor

After eating too many raspberry tarts, the princess declares that if she can have the moon she will be well again. The wisdom of the royal advisors fails. The common sense of the jester prevails. Washes of pinks and blues complement the whimsy of the humorous fantasy.

HONORS

A Child's Good Night Book by Margaret Wise Brown, illustrated by Jean Charlot. W. R. SCOTT.

Crayon drawings

Night has come and everything is going to sleep. Animals, children, and even engines are sleepy. The brief story ends with a prayer to bless and guard "small things that have no words." The repetitious phrases and drawings are designed to bring on drowsiness.

The Good-Luck Horse by Chih-Yi Chan, illustrated by Plato Chan. WHITTLESEY.

Pen and ink; wash (?)

A lonely boy in ancient China creates a very small paper horse that he can hold in his hand. Magically the horse becomes real. Although the magician names it "Good-Luck Horse," the story proves that sometimes good luck is bad luck and vice versa. The adventures of the horse are re-created in the line and wash drawings.

The Mighty Hunter **by Berta and Elmer Hader, illustrated by the authors. MACMILLAN.**

Watercolor

Little Brave Heart's mother tells him to go to school so he can grow up to be a wise leader, but he goes hunting instead. Each animal in turn tells him that there is a better animal to shoot. The bear chastises him for hunting for "fun," and chases him to school. The illustrations alternate between black-and-white and desert colors.

Small Rain: Verses from the Bible, **chosen by Jessie Orton Jones, illustrated by Elizabeth Orton Jones. VIKING.**

Medium not known

Brief Bible verses taken from the King James Version of the Old and New Testaments are illustrated with children doing everyday things—romping, playing, sitting quietly, sharing, running, crying, and sleeping. Each verse relates in some way to what the children are doing.

Pierre Pidgeon **by Lee Kingman, illustrated by Arnold Edwin Bare. HOUGHTON MIFFLIN.**

Preseparated gouache and ink drawings

Seven-year-old Pierre has long been fascinated by the boat-in-bottle in the shop. Finally he purchases it, and before he gets it home he breaks it. Studying the broken model, he succeeds in figuring out how the boat got into the bottle. Gray, green, and peach tones reflect a Canadian fishing village.

1943 AWARD

The Little House **by Virginia Lee Burton, illustrated by the author. HOUGHTON MIFFLIN.**

Watercolor

Built long ago far out in the country, the Little House is now surrounded by the city. Circular shapes abound in the illustrations and the lines of type. Bright, happy colors give way to dark, moody ones as progress overtakes the house. Light colors return when the house is moved to a new countryside.

HONORS

Dash and Dart **by Mary and Conrad Buff, illustrated by the authors. VIKING.**

Lithographs (?)

In simple, poetic text and mood-capturing sepia paintings, the first year in the life of two fawns is described. A great reverence for nature is felt throughout the book.

Marshmallow by Clare Turlay Newberry, illustrated by the author. HARPER.

Charcoal (?)

Oliver the cat lives a blissful life of eating and sleeping until the lady who takes care of him brings home a bundle of live, soft fur. Suddenly Oliver is terrified when he is confronted with a bunny named Marshmallow. The pictures show how their relationship grows until they both curl up together.

1942 AWARD

Make Way for Ducklings by Robert McCloskey, illustrated by the author. VIKING.

Lithographic crayon on stone

Having hatched her ducklings and taught them to march nicely in single file, Mrs. Mallard decides to take them straight through Boston's busy streets to their new home in the Public Garden and pond. Sketchy brown drawings humorously show the ordeal the mallards face.

HONORS

In My Mother's House by Ann Nolan Clark, illustrated by Velino Herrera. VIKING.

Medium not known

Daily life of the pueblo as seen through the eyes of the children is described in a rhythmic, simple prose. Many aspects of life—houses, food, clothing, and agriculture—are pictured. Tribal designs and pen-and-ink and color drawings depict the Tawa life.

Nothing at All by Wanda Gág, illustrated by the author. COWARD.

Original lithographs in color

Three orphan dogs, two visible and one invisible, are adopted by two children. It takes a jackdaw, some magic, and a lot of energetic work by Nothing At All to become Something After All. Intriguing, lightly colored lithographs show the invisible become visible.

Paddle-to-the-Sea by Holling Clancy Holling, illustrated by the author. HOUGHTON MIFFLIN.

Full-color oil paintings

In the Canadian wilderness, a young boy carves a canoe with an Indian figure seated in it, then launches it from Lake Nipigon. The text and illustrations are filled with information about the scenes the canoe passes, from the quiet byways, to a sawmill, to a raging forest fire.

An American ABC by Maud and Miska Petersham, illustrated by the authors. MACMILLAN.

Pencil and preseparated watercolor

Familiar symbols, historic places, and legendary figures form the basis of this patriotic interpretation of the alphabet. Decorated in red, white, blue, and black, each letter provides a brief lesson in American history. The strength and courage of those who shaped America are visible in the drawings.

1941 AWARD

They Were Strong and Good by Robert Lawson, illustrated by the author. VIKING.

Brush and ink

Writing of his mother and father and their mothers and fathers, Lawson says they, like the ancestors of many others, were never famous but were "strong and good" and helped to build America. Line-and-brush drawings are sometimes humorous but more often depict the strength and goodness of the land and its people.

HONOR

April's Kittens by Clare Turlay Newberry, illustrated by the author. HARPER.

Ink, charcoal, and watercolor

After her cat has kittens, April must decide on the one cat to keep. Illustrations of the black cats make them look fuzzy and furry. Occasional touches of red add a dash of color.

1940 AWARD

Abraham Lincoln by Ingri and Edgar Parin d'Aulaire, illustrated by the authors. DOUBLEDAY, DORAN.

Lithographic pencil on stone

Well-known anecdotes of Lincoln, particularly of his youth and prairie years, are recounted with strength and humor in this picture biography. Lithographs in color and black and white reveal details of American life in the 1800s.

Published with new text and completely new illustrations in 1957 (Doubleday).

HONORS

Madeline by Ludwig Bemelmans, illustrated by the author. SIMON & SCHUSTER.

Brush, pen, and watercolor (?)

High-spirited Madeline may be the smallest of the twelve little girls at Miss Clavel's school, but she is by far the bravest. Lilting rhythmic text and simple, childlike paintings provide a tour of Paris and introduce a spunky heroine.

The Ageless Story **by Lauren Ford with its Antiphons pictured by the author. DODD, MEAD.**

Painting; touches of gold leaf (?)

The story of the Christ Child is told through Gregorian music, biblical text, and illustrations that are an adaptation of illuminated manuscripts. The illustrations are a blend of early Renaissance religious art in a New England setting.

Cock-a-Doodle-Doo **by Berta and Elmer Hader, illustrated by the authors. MACMILLAN.**

Watercolor

In a reversal of the story of the Ugly Duckling, a chick is hatched by a duck. The ducklings make fun of him, and soon the chick goes off in search of others like him. In alternating color and black-and-white pictures he faces several perils before landing in the hen house.

1939 AWARD

Mei Li **by Thomas Handforth, illustrated by the author. DOUBLEDAY, DORAN.**

Brush and lithograph pencil (?)

The New Year Fair is in the city, and Mei Li's brother has been told that he can go, but little girls have to stay home. Strong, bold line drawings present many aspects of Chinese culture and customs as they follow the irrepressible Mei Li, who sneaks off for a grand time at the fair.

HONORS

The Forest Pool **by Laura Adams Armer, illustrated by the author. LONGMANS, GREEN.**

Medium not known

Glowing with the bright golden colors of South America, stylized pictures show two boys as they go in search of the iguana in the bell-flower tree. The boys ponder the animals that know so much but never reveal their secrets.

Andy and the Lion **by James Daugherty, illustrated by the author. VIKING.**

Charcoal rubbed off on light gray transfer and rubbed in (?)

The old story of Androcles and the lion is retold in a modern setting. Andy signs out a book about lions from the library. The next day he comes upon a lion with a thorn stuck in his paw. Told and illustrated with robust tall-tale humor, the twists of the tale lead to a fine friendship.

Snow White and the Seven Dwarfs, **translated and illustrated by Wanda Gág.** COWARD.

Lithographs (?)

In this little book the Brothers Grimm story of the vain, wicked stepmother, the seven dwarfs, and the beautiful princess is retold with much repetition. The black-and-white drawings are filled with rounded shapes that continue the repetitiousness of the story.

Wee Gillis **by Munro Leaf, illustrated by Robert Lawson.** VIKING.

Drawings in pen and tempera

The Highland relatives want Wee Gillis to stalk stags with them. The Lowland relatives want him to tend the cows. After years of doing both, Wee Gillis has powerful lungs from calling the cows, and he has learned to sit very still from stalking stags—just the skills needed to play a bagpipe! Line drawings sparkle with humorous spirit.

Barkis **by Clare Turlay Newberry, illustrated by the author.** HARPER.

Charcoal pencil and watercolor wash

A bickering brother and sister squabble over the ownership of a new puppy and cat. They finally reach a solution that makes them both happy. Soft brown-and-black drawings of the winsome cat and dog are set against white backgrounds.

1938 AWARD

Animals of the Bible: A Picture Book, **text from the King James Bible selected by Helen Dean Fish, illustrated by Dorothy P. Lathrop.** STOKES.

Black-and-white lithographs

The Old and New Testaments of the King James Version are the sources for thirty-one stories about animals. Black-and-white full-page illustrations include the flora of biblical lands and portray the animals with reverence.

Published with revised art after 1937 (Stokes).

HONORS

Seven Simeons: A Russian Tale, **retold and illustrated by Boris Artzybasheff.** VIKING.

Pen and ink

King Douda, wise, rich, strong, and very handsome, decides to marry a princess as beautiful as himself. To help him in his quest, he engages seven brothers, each of whom has a special skill that, by the tale's end, is used in a most unusual manner. Love triumphs in the end in this whimsically decorated book with neat color line drawings.

Four and Twenty Blackbirds: Nursery Rhymes of Yesterday Recalled for Children of Today, **collected by Helen Dean Fish, illustrated by Robert Lawson. STOKES.**

Drawings in pen and tempera

The twenty-four nursery rhymes found here were culled from out-of-print books or "rescued from memories of older people." Most are long and filled with the jingling and sturdy humor of traditional nursery rhymes. They are illustrated with vigorous drawings in black and green. Simple music is given for those rhymes that have tunes.

Author/Illustrator Index

A

Aardema, Verna, 132
Ackerman, Karen, 122
Adams, Adrienne, 142, 144
Adams, Helen Simmons (as Nancy Barnes), 70
Adams, Julia Davis, 85, 87
Alexander, Kwame, 20
Alexander, Lloyd, 52, 55, 91
Alger, Leclaire (as Sorche Nic Leodhas), 56, 139, 141
Allee, Marjorie, 84
Allen, Rick, 24
Andersen, Hans Christian, 148
Angelo, Valenti, 77, 78
Appelt, Kathi, 25
Applegate, Katherine, 22
Armer, Laura Adams, 84, 163
Armer, Sidney, 84
Armstrong, Alan, 27
Armstrong, William H., 52
Arthur, Malcolm, 120
Artzybasheff, Boris, 75, 89, 164
Atwater, Florence, 77
Atwater, Richard, 77
Avi, 30, 38
Azarian, Mary, 113

B

Babbitt, Natalie, 51
Bahti, Tom, 134
Bailey, Carolyn Sherwin, 70
Baity, Elizabeth, 65
Baker, Olaf, 127
Bang, Molly, 112, 126, 128
Bannon, Laura, 78
Bare, Arnold Edwin, 160
Barkley, James, 52
Barnes, Nancy, pseud. (Helen Simmons Adams), 70
Barnett, Mac, 97, 100
Barney, Maginel Wright, 89
Barnum, Jay Hyde, 156
Bartoletti, Susan Campbell, 28

Bartone, Elisa, 117
Baskin, Hosea, 134
Baskin, Leonard, 134
Baskin, Lisa, 134
Baskin, Tobias, 134
Bauer, Joan, 31
Bauer, Marion Dane, 40
Baylor, Byrd, 130, 131, 132, 134
Becker, Aaron, 99
Beddows, Eric, 39
Bell, Cece, 21
Belting, Natalia M., 142
Bemelmans, Ludwig, 79, 148, 162
Bennett, John, 88
Bernstein, Zena, 50
Berry, Erick, pseud. (Allena Best), 81, 82, 85
Best, Allena (as Erick Berry), 81, 82, 85
Best, Herbert, 85
Besterman, Catherine, 69
Bianco, Margery, 79
Bileck, Marvin, 140
Bing, Christopher, 111
Birch, Reginald, 92
Birnbaum, Abe, 148
Bishop, Claire Huchet, 63, 69
Bjorklund, Lorence, 64
Black, Holly, 21
Blair, Helen, 71
Blegvad, Erik, 45, 59
Bloom, Lloyd, 42
Blos, Joan W., 45
Blumberg, Rhoda, 41
Bock, Vera, 87
Bolognese, Don, 54
Bond, Nancy, 47
Bontemps, Arna, 68
Bowen, William, 92
Bowman, James Cloyd, 78
Boyle, Mildred, 73, 75, 76, 78
Brink, Carol Ryrie, 80
Brittain, Bill, 42
Brooks, Bruce, 37, 41

Title Index